SONNY SIXKILLER'S TALES FROM THE HUSKIES SIDELINE

Sonny Sixkiller
with
Bob Condotta

www.SportsPublishingLLC.com

ISBN: 1-58261-407-5

Interior photos: © University of Washington

Publisher: Peter L. Bannon
Senior managing editor: Susan M. Moyer
Acquisitions editor: Mike Pearson
Developmental editor: Kipp Wilfong
Cover/dust jacket design: Dustin Hubbart
Project manager: Alicia Wentworth
Imaging: Kenneth J. O'Brien, Christine Mohrbacher
Copy editor: Cynthia L. McNew
Photo editor: Erin Linden-Levy
Vice president of sales and marketing: Kevin King
Media and promotions managers: Nick Obradovich (regional),
    Randy Fouts (national), Maurey Williamson (print)

Printed in the United States of America

Sports Publishing L.L.C.
804 North Neil Street
Champaign, IL 61820

Phone: 1-877-424-2665
Fax: 217-363-2073
Web site: www.SportsPublishingLLC.com

Dedicated to Huskies everywhere—once a Dawg, always a Dawg!

—Sonny Sixkiller

Dedicated to my father, Denny Louis Condotta, who instilled in me a love of sports, reading and writing and the ability to somehow merge the three into a career.

—Bob Condotta

CONTENTS

Preface...vii
Acknowledgments ix
Introduction..................................xi

CHAPTER 1
  Starting Out 1

CHAPTER 2
  The Coaches 23

CHAPTER 3
  The Quarterbacks......................... 43

CHAPTER 4
  The Big Games........................... 66

CHAPTER 5
  Some of My Favorite Players................ 85

CHAPTER 6
  Unsung Heroes......................... 111

CHAPTER 7
  Friends and Rivals 130

Epilogue 145

PREFACE

The state of Washington was officially chartered on November 11, 1889.

Seventeen days later, the University of Washington played its first football game.

And thus started one of the state's great traditions—Husky football—even if the team wouldn't be named the Huskies for 33 years (the team was called the Sun Dodgers until the school decided to change the name in 1921).

Though the Huskies lost that first game 7-0 to a group of alumni of Ivy League schools living in the area, they have won more often than not ever since.

Entering the 2004 season, the Washington Huskies have won 638 games and lost just 353, ranking among the top 15 in the nation in winning percentage.

The Huskies have also played in 30 bowl games, second most in the Pac-10, including 14 Rose Bowls, and their 63-game non-losing streak from 1907-1917 is the longest in the history of college football.

Those numbers alone say it all about the great tradition of Husky football.

But Washington football is about more than win-loss records or championships.

It is about the feeling of 72,500 fans packed into Husky Stadium on a blustery November Seattle day watching the home team beat up on a resigned visitor.

It is about the great coaches—Dobie, Owens and James—and players—McElhenny, Moon and Tuiasosopo—who have roamed the sidelines.

Mostly, it is about a love affair between a team and its fans, among the most rabid in the history of the game.

In these pages, one of the greatest of all Huskies— quarterback Sonny Sixkiller—takes you through some of the great players, coaches, games and moments in the history of the Washington football program with a special emphasis on his own sterling career.

Sixkiller was so popular during his three years as UW's starting QB from 1970-72 that there were songs written in his honor and T-shirts made in his image. He remains the last Husky featured on the cover of *Sports Illustrated*.

And when the Huskies celebrated 100 years of football in 1990, it was written by one observer that Sixkiller "may have been the most popular Husky of the century."

Since leaving UW, he has remained close to the program, serving for the last 10 years as the color analyst for Husky football games on Fox Sports Northwest.

So sit back and enjoy as Sixkiller takes you through the history of the Huskies as he has seen it.

ACKNOWLEDGMENTS

The authors would like to thank Jim Daves and the University of Washington sports information department and Mike Reagan of the UW trademarks and licensing department. Also, the authors would like to acknowledge the work of authors who have previously written about the history of UW football, notably Steve Rudman and Dick Rockne, as well as the assistance of the archives of *The Seattle Times*.

INTRODUCTION

Funny thing about my name. My given first name is Alex.

But I was almost always called Sonny. I had a grandmother who originally called me "Sonny Boy" when I was a little kid and it just stuck. I've been Sonny ever since.

It's kind of bizarre, but in the early days of the University of Washington—before the 1920s—the UW's football mascot was a three and a half-foot wooden statue of the happy-faced character, Sunny, who appeared in the school's humor magazine, at the time called the *Sun Dodger*.

I actually never knew that until I came to Washington, but I guess it shows I was destined to be a Husky.

UW changed its mascot in 1923, and Sunny disappeared and was not discovered until 23 years later in South Bend, Indiana, where it had been taken by a prankster and kept in hiding. He was given back to UW in 1948 and displayed at the UW Alumni Association. He was abducted again in the spring of 1994 in what was thought to be a fraternity prank. But he was found a couple of days later in Issaquah, a suburb of Seattle, and now resides in the Husky Hall of Fame. Since I have a spot there as well, I guess you can say there are two "Sunny Boys" in the Husky Hall of Fame.

In the song that was written about me in 1971, "The Ballad of Sonny Sixkiller," there's a line that says "He grew up the proud grandson of an Indian chief."

That's true, I did.

But my upbringing was no different than that of millions of other young boys who grew up in the 1950s and 1960s.

When I was one year old, my family moved from Oklahoma to Ashland, Oregon, when my father got a new job. My family had moved to Oklahoma in 1838 after the Trail of Tears incident when Indians were forcibly relocated from Georgia and the Carolinas.

And it was there in Ashland that my love of sports—and football—began. Everybody always talks about playing sandlot baseball, and we did that a lot. But we used to spend hours playing pickup football.

Football had run in our family. My brother John—he was six years older than me—had played high school ball. When I was a kid, I used to sneak into games and stand on the sidelines. Sometimes I'd hold the down markers. There were a few games where I held the sticks and watched Bill Enyart—who went on to become a legend at Oregon State—play for Medford High, one of our rivals. He was the biggest high school player I'd ever seen. He was just huge.

When I was five, I got run over by a few players and split my lip real bad. Some of the guys on the team carried me home, and I'll never forget the look on my mom's face when she saw me. But that's how it was in Ashland.

I first became aware of what Washington Husky football meant while sitting in the living room of my home in

Ashland, Oregon, in 1968, watching a game on TV with my father.

There was this great panoramic view of Husky Stadium sitting on the waters of Lake Washington, which remains to me one of the greatest sights in all of sports.

I remember seeing Jim Owens manning the sidelines wearing his sunglasses and all those purple helmets running around. It was a sight I couldn't believe.

The Huskies played Cal that day, I think, and Al Worley intercepted a pass on his way to setting an NCAA record with 14 picks that year. Worley, so aptly nicknamed "The Thief," finished his career with 18 interceptions, still the most in school history.

I remember telling my dad, "That's where I want to play football."

Of course, I didn't know if I would have that opportunity. Though I was listed as weighing 160 pounds when I was a senior in high school, I was actually just 153—spread over all of five feet, 10 inches. I was a pretty skinny kid—they used to call me wiry, and that might almost have been stretching the truth.

But I had an in when it came to Washington.

Another former Ashland High great, Gene Willis, had headed north to UW to play quarterback two years earlier. When he was home on vacations, I would talk to him about what it was like playing for the Huskies. Those conversations just whetted my appetite.

Fortunately, a local scout named Earl Nordvedt, a former Husky baseball player who was based in northern California and had also helped send Willis to UW, had his eyes on me my senior year and told the UW coaches they should take a look.

Eventually, the Huskies decided to take Nordvedt's advice and assistant coach Bob Schloredt—himself one of the greatest Husky QBs of all time, leading the 1959 team to a Rose Bowl title—paid my high school a visit.

I remember that visit like it was right out of the movies. Here comes this big ol' guy, and just looking at him, it was obvious that he was somebody.

Remember, Ashland is a small town—even today it has a population of just about 20,000. It wasn't every day that former All-American quarterbacks came to town, even if I had no idea who Schloredt was at the time.

I remember when he got up to leave, my head coach, John Buck, told me that was Bob Schloredt, the one-eyed QB who had led the Huskies to the Rose Bowl. He asked me if I knew who he was, and I said, 'Nope.' I had no idea.

But as things progressed, he came down again to see me play basketball, and he said he liked the way I moved and saw some ability. That's when the Huskies got serious.

The next time Bob Schloredt came down, he brought Jim Owens with him. It was so weird. I was there with my mom and dad thinking about all the things that I liked about UW. I knew how big the school was, how beautiful it was, what an opportunity it would be to play at a big institution like that and play in the Pac-8 Conference against USC and Cal and all those teams I saw on TV.

I felt good about the meeting.

But years later, Coach Schloredt told me that as they were leaving the house, Owens hit him on the arm and said, "Man, is that kid going to grow?" Schloredt said, "I don't care. He can throw the ball."

My decision was clinched after I made a recruiting trip to Seattle. I took the first plane ride of my life for my official recruiting visit, along with another local player, going on a little prop airplane from Medford to Portland and Portland to Seattle. I had made a decision that would change my life—to become a Washington Husky.

Chapter 1
STARTING OUT

A UW Career Begins

Little did I know when I showed up for my freshman year at the University of Washington that there would be about 12 quarterbacks on the roster and that we were going to change the offense to run the wishbone. I wondered for a while what I had gotten myself into.

We didn't redshirt as freshmen back then, as they do now, or play on the varsity. That was back in the days of freshman ineligibility.

Instead, we played our own schedule against freshmen from other schools, like Washington State, which was our first game of the season.

When the game started, Calvin Jones, who would go on to be an All-American, forgot to catch the opening kickoff. It landed at like the five-yard line and went into the end zone. The Cougars pounced on it and scored. No time off the clock and we were down 7-0.

Sonny Sixkiller

It got worse. There were a lot of good players on that WSU team with whom we would have a good rivalry for the next few years, like Ty Paine and Bill Moos—who is now the athletic director at Oregon—and we lost 45-7.

And that was my welcome to big-time college football.

The "Moroccan Mole"

The coach of that freshman team was Marv Weetman. Mac Bledsoe—Drew Bledsoe's dad, who had played at UW in the 1960s—was also one of our coaches, and so was Al Worley.

But it was Weetman's team. And he was a guy you couldn't really dislike. He was bald and wore Coke-bottle glasses and talked like he was a real tough guy and looked like a mole. So Ron Shepherd, a linebacker and one of the cooler guys on the team, nicknamed him the "Moroccan Mole."

Anyway, the Monday after that loss to WSU, Weetman came out and went through the classic General Patton kind of thing. Everyone was on pins and needles. He goes through every player, telling a receiver, "If someone asks you why we didn't throw the ball to you, tell them it's because you can't catch it." He tells the linemen, "If someone asks you why we didn't run the ball, tell them it's because you can't block."

He went through every guy like that. And then we go and work out and it's doubles of everything. Double jumping jacks. Double up-downs. Every drill there is.

At one point, we did a drill that came to be known as the Burma Road. They'd put a tackling dummy every five yards up and down the field—alternating putting them on the yardline and the hash mark. We had to go up and down the field, 100 yards, in full gear, and then turn around and do it again.

The Turning Point

As tough as that day was, however, I think that was the turning point for that era of Husky football.

The 1969 team lost its first nine games, and the wishbone wasn't looking like such a good idea. When we got crushed in our first game, they kind of changed things to more of a drop-back passing offense for the freshman team. I got the start the next week at Oregon and we won, and that was the end of the wishbone. We never saw it again, at least for our class.

Our freshman team finished that season 3-1, and then we went up to help the varsity. We had been kind of distanced from them up until then and didn't really know what was going on with them. If you remember, that was the season of the black player revolt, and things got kind of ugly for a while.

I still remember being at the Tubby Graves Building doing a Reading Dynamics Course the Friday before the UCLA game and then going down to wish the team good luck at the Crew House. I look around and I'm thinking, "Where's Lee Brock? Where's Ralph Bayard?" (They were among about a dozen black players who didn't make the trip for the game in protest against what they felt were racist actions by coach Jim Owens.) I had no clue what was going on, because as freshmen, we were pretty removed from all of that.

I grew up in the 1960s, and for me, it was a time of fun. We didn't have a lot of stuff like this going on in Ashland. Then you come up to a big city like Seattle and you see all of that going on and you think, "Wow, this is really something of a social event." I remember walking back and thinking, "Man, what's going to happen now?"

The Season Ends on a Good Note

When we went up to practice with the varsity, it was like we were getting the frustration of the season taken out on us. I remember Lee Brock, who was one of the captains on that team, just nailing me in practice. Lee was a hard-rushing defensive end from Seattle and many times he would just hit me and I would literally roll back over the end zone. Greg Collins was the other freshman quarterback, and he was just handing off to the running backs. I remember yelling to him, "Hey, Collins, it's time to switch so I can hand off for a while."

But I think we really helped the varsity. We had a pretty good base of talent and ability, and I think we had a lot to do with helping them win their last game that year. We were 0-9 and WSU was 1-8 going into the Apple Cup. But despite everything that had happened that season, the varsity was able to beat the Cougars 30-21—the only time all season the varsity scored more than 14 points in a game.

It was a sign of things to come.

Greg Collins

Having Second Thoughts

It may seem now like there was never a question that I would become a starting quarterback for the Huskies.

But it almost never happened.

In fact, I had to get talked into sticking around the program at the end of that freshman season. I didn't really feel like the coaches were in tune with me, even though I did pretty well as a freshman. They really liked Greg Collins, who was from Torrance, California, and they should have.

Nothing against him—he was a really good quarterback who lettered from 1970-72.

Gene Willis, my old friend from Ashland, became my roommate at UW. One day, he told me that the coaches had asked him to work out with Greg Collins and they didn't want me to know. He did the workout without telling me.

I thought, "If that's the way they are going to do things, that's fine, that's cool." I really thought about saying, "That's it." I'd had a bad first quarter in the classroom and moved out of the frats so I could study, and I was thinking maybe this wasn't meant to be.

But there was a basketball team for some of the football players that winter—we would go play the faculty and lettermen's clubs, things like that—and I really got to know a lot of the other guys on the team, like Bo Cornell and Bob Burmeister and Danny Roberson. That really helped a lot.

I remember it was building those relationships and talking it out with those guys that convinced me to hold on through spring ball.

A Little Luck

Staying was the best move I ever made.

I was still buried on the depth chart heading into the spring of 1970, entering my sophomore year. But then

Gene Willis got hurt, and Steve Hanzlik, who had lettered at QB in 1969, decided to play baseball instead.

All of the sudden, I'm getting a few more turns in practice every day.

We used to play the spring game every year against the alumni. That year, that meant playing against a lot of guys who were in the NFL at the time, like Ben Davidson, who was then starring with the Oakland Raiders, and Ron Medved, then with the Philadelphia Eagles.

I remember saying before the spring game, "I don't know if I'm ready."

But that game was a lot of fun. That was a good team for us to play against—we were so tired of playing against ourselves by that point because spring ball lasted a lot longer than it does now.

Greg Collins started the game, but he hurt his shoulder on the second series, and Coach Owens said, "Where's Sixkiller?" I thought to myself, "Hey, this is my shot. Let's go."

I played the rest of the game, completing 24-50 passes for 389 yards, and running wild back there and just throwing the ball all over the place. I remember the alumni guys coming up after the game saying, "Man, that was amazing."

A Spartan Beginning

I held onto the starting job heading into the 1970 season. We opened at home against Michigan State, a team that had beaten us 27-11 the year before, the first of nine straight defeats for the 1969 team.

Michigan State wasn't quite the powerhouse that it had been a few years before—the Spartans had gone 4-6 the year before.

Still, almost everyone outside of Husky Stadium figured they'd beat us, considering we had gone 1-9 the year before and now were starting a sophomore quarterback who had never played a down of varsity football before.

We got the ball first and on first down, I threw a pass to Ace Bulger, our senior tight end, over the middle. The crowd went nuts. Remember, we had been a wishbone team the year before, and Coach Owens had a reputation for being a three-yards-and-a-cloud-of-dust kind of guy.

But here we were throwing the ball one play into the season.

After a Bo Cornell run, it was third down. I dropped back for a pass and all of the sudden, the middle of the field opened up just like an ocean. I took off, and I remember thinking, "Here I am, running down the middle of the field at Husky Stadium." It was just so loud. I was thinking, "Oh my God, I'm not used to this."

A few plays later, I threw my first touchdown pass. It was a play-action pass, and Ira Hammon, a split end from Portland, ran a post and up. I hit him for about a 30-yard touchdown.

I still get chills sitting here thinking about it all these years later.

Anyway, we ended up beating the Spartans 42-16, the most points the Huskies had scored since the first game of the 1960 season.

We lost the next week to Michigan, 17-3, but then the next week we beat Navy, 56-7, and it was becoming evident to everyone that things were changing.

Becoming 6 Killer

It might seem like it always made sense for me to wear the No. 6, given my name.

But believe it or not, I had never worn No. 6 until I got to the University of Washington.

At my high school, quarterbacks wore No. 12 and No. 15, so that's what I wore.

And I didn't even wear No. 6 as a freshman at UW. I think I was either 10 or 11. I just never thought about wearing No. 6, even though it seems obvious now because of my name.

But it was John Reid, who was then the sports information director at UW and went on to become one of the main organizers of the Holiday Bowl, who convinced the UW coaches that I should wear No. 6.

What a great move that was.

The Payback Game

One of my favorite wins that year came against UCLA late in the season, actually our last home game of the year.

UCLA had beaten us 57-14 the year before, the game most memorable for the black player revolt.

That was the worst loss Coach Owens ever suffered during his Husky coaching career, which lasted from 1957-74.

But that wasn't the worst of it.

Those of us who weren't with the team that day were watching the game on TV. I remember it was something like 45-7 in the second half. You might have thought that UCLA coach Tommy Prothro would have taken it a little easy on us, knowing that we were having a bad year and that a bunch of our key players weren't even there.

Instead, he pulled a trick play where a guy acts like he's running off the field and then they snap the ball and throw it to him for a touchdown. We don't have a lot of our best players and they run it up on us? That's BS.

The next year, we couldn't wait for UCLA to come to town.

And they weren't bad that season. They were ranked No. 17 when we played them, having beaten Washington State 54-9 the week before. They had a lot of good players, like Dave Dalby, who went onto a long career with the Raiders.

But we were fired up and played our best game of the year. We threw the ball at will all game.

I completed 18-35 passes for three touchdowns and 277 yards. Jim Krieg caught eight passes for 145 yards and Al Mauer caught four passes for 140 yards and three touchdowns. Greg Collins came in and threw three touchdown passes of his own—the six we combined for was still a school record entering the 2004 season. We ended up winning 61-20.

But that's not what most people remember most about that game.

Everyone remembered how UCLA ran it up on us the year before. So even though we had a huge lead late in the game, we pulled an on-side kick late in the game. I remember Prothro taking off his hat and throwing it down. The wind caught it, and it went on the field. We were just laughing our tails off. Yeah, payback is a good feeling.

We finished that season with 43-25 win over Washington State in Spokane the week after the UCLA game to conclude what had been one of Washington's best seasons in years.

Boiling Over

Based on our 1970 season, there was a lot of excitement heading into 1971.

After we beat UC-Santa Barbara 65-7 in our opener—incredibly, the Gauchos scored first to put a quick scare into us before we "rallied"—we hosted Purdue.

I always liked playing Big Ten teams during my career. Those games create great rivalries, and I just had a feeling heading into this one that it would be a hot game.

Come game day, it was indeed hot—85-90 degrees on one of those perfect Seattle September days. On that old Husky Stadium astrotruf, it felt like 100 degrees. The game was on national TV, and Purdue was the biggest team I remember seeing, and talented too, guys who played a long time in the NFL, like Gary Danielson, Otis Armstrong, Dave Butz and Darryl Stingley.

The game went back and forth, and we were trailing 35-31 when we got the ball back late in the game. On a third-and-six play with about three minutes to go, I hit Tommy Scott for the go-ahead touchdown. They got the ball back and drove down the field, but then Rick Huget intercepted a pass to seal the victory.

That was a major turning point for our team. The following week, we were ranked No. 17 in the country, the first time the Huskies had been in the top 20 since 1964.

Raindrops Keep Falling...

The next week we hosted TCU on a Saturday when it rained more than I ever remember seeing at Husky Stadium.

It rained so hard we didn't even go out for the pregame warmups. We waited until the storm passed through and then went out. The field looked like it had glazed-on ice on it because it was raining so hard.

We won 44-26 in the kind of shootout that was becoming common for us.

At one point, they ran a kickoff back for a touchdown. Then Jim Kreig turned right around and ran their kickoff all the way back. I had never seen that before.

Fighting the Illini

We had one non-conference game left that season against Illinois in Champaign. They had obviously heard that we were a fast team that liked to throw the ball, because when we showed up, the grass on the field was a foot and a half tall. I'd never seen grass that high before.

We were favored to win, but the whole first half, we couldn't get untracked. It was 7-7 late in the second quarter, and we were driving for a touchdown when Tommy Scott didn't block the end man on a little quick goal line pass.

I got hit from behind and they intercepted and ran it back 99 yards for a touchdown. We were down 14-7 at halftime.

There wasn't much to say at halftime; we just needed to go back out there and start turning things around.

And did we ever. We ended up winning 52-14, scoring 42 points in the second half, which is still tied for the school record for the most points scored in a second half (it also happened in 1974 against Oregon).

We got 28 of those points in the fourth quarter, still the second most points scored in a fourth quarter in school history (we had scored 30 in that payback game against UCLA the year before).

As you might expect, we were feeling good after the game.

Getting the Cover of *Sports Illustrated*

Our 4-0 start combined with our exciting play began to garner us a lot of attention.

It was after the TCU game that Mark Lookabaugh, who was the sports information director back then, asked me if I wanted to be on the cover of *Sports Illustrated*.

Being on the cover of *SI* is still about the most noteriety you can get as an athlete. But it was an even bigger deal back then before there was ESPN, *USA Today* and all kinds of other media outlets. Back then, *Sports Illustrated* was about all there was.

It would obviously be a great honor.

But I told them that I didn't really want to be on the cover, that it would be a distraction for the team and all that stuff. But they told me about what great exposure it would be for the program, how much good it would do for me and everybody involved.

I remember after a practice Mark came to me and said, "I want you to meet somebody." It was Roy Blount Jr., with *Sports Illustrated*.

The *SI* Jinx

The issue came out the Monday before we played Stanford, a game that loomed large in our chances to go to the Rose Bowl, as the Cardinal—though they were still called the Indians at the time—had gone the year before.

And if you looked at their coaching staff, you knew why. Not only was John Ralston their head coach, but they had a great assistant coaching staff that included guys like George Seifert.

It was just a crazy environment for that game. We had a crowd of 60,777 in the old configuration at Husky Stadium, which was the largest attendance the Huskies had ever had.

If only the game had been as good.

That Stanford defense, which was nicknamed the Thunder Chickens, was really something, with guys like Benny Barnes and Jeff Siemon who played in the NFL for a long time. I think nine of their 11 starters played in the pros.

I just never had time to throw, and we couldn't run the ball—we had just one rushing first down all day, which at the time tied a school record. I'd never seen the corner blitzes and stuff that they threw at us. I have to say that we got outcoached—we weren't prepared for the game and had never seen a defense like that.

We lost 17-6, a defeat that basically kept us out of the Rose Bowl.

Falling Just Short

Of course, the one thing we didn't do during that time was go to a Rose Bowl. Or any bowl at all. That was during the time when only the conference champion made it to a bowl game. That made motivation hard sometimes if you knew you were out of it.

That 1971 season was our best chance. We finished 8-3 and outscored our opponents 357-182, for the second straight year setting a school record for points in a season—it wasn't broken until the 1984 team went 11-1 and won the Orange Bowl.

The Stanford game, the week after the *SI* cover, was the most crucial defeat.

But our other two losses might have been even tougher to take.

The week after the Stanford game, we traveled to Eugene and took an early 14-0 lead on the Ducks. We had a chance to go up 21-0, but a touchdown got called back by a penalty. As so often happens in those kinds of situations, we ended up turning the ball over on a fumble and the Ducks took over the momentum.

We were trailing 23-21 late in the game when we drove down the field and had a chance to kick a short field goal to win the game. But the kick went right over the top of the goal post and was ruled no good. To lose like that was just horrible, even if it was a good Oregon team that had Dan Fouts at quarterback and Bobby Moore (who later changed his name to Ahmad Rashad) at running back.

A couple weeks later we hosted USC. We were up 12-10 with about three minutes to go in the game. On a third and eight we decided to pass the ball rather than run it and punt and let our defense hold them, as it had been doing all game. I threw a pass that bounced off Jim Kreig's shoulder pads and was picked off by Artemis Spears—the kind of thing you've seen a million times. They went down and kicked a field goal, and we lost 13-12, just another devastating defeat.

That's always been one of my biggest what-ifs. What if we had run the ball? What if I had thrown the pass just a little lower? We never did beat USC in my time as a Husky.

The White Shoes Game

The season ended happily a week later, however, with a 28-20 win over Washington State that gave us our best record since the 1960 team that won the Rose Bowl.

That's not what most of us remember about that game, however.

That was back when wearing white shoes was all the rage, like Joe Namath and Billy "White Shoes" Johnson. And we wanted to join in the fad.

Coach Owens, however, wanted us to wear black shoes. We went out for warmups in the black shoes, but then we went in and we all taped our shoes so that when we came back out for the kickoff, we were all in white. You should have heard the crowd—everyone seemed to think it was really funny.

The only problem was it was raining like mad, and as the day wore on, all the tape started wearing off and was strewn all over the field. It became a real mess.

Good thing we won the game.

Boiling Over (Again)

The next year, my senior season, we started out 2-0 when we headed back to Purdue for a rematch against the Boilermakers.

People ask me all the time what was my favorite game or best game or most memorable game, and they have to be the two we played against Purdue.

We had won in a close one at home in 1971, and now we had to go back to Ross-Ade Stadium, which is not a pretty place to play. I remember Coach Owens got hit with a chunk of ice—the fans are right on top of you there. So he told us to make sure we kept our "head gear" on all game. That's what he always said—head gear. He didn't call them helmets.

The first half was all Purdue. With the option, quarterback Gary Danielson was running wild, and we had some pretty disgruntled players on our sidelines because we felt we were running the wrong defenses. We wanted to run just our base defense instead of a bunch of other stuff. Danielson had 200 yards at halftime (he finished with 213, the most ever by a quarterback against the Huskies).

But then he cramped up and couldn't play a lot of the second half.

We were down 21-0 at halftime, and as we headed to our locker room, we had to cross right through the Purdue players.

Boy, were they in my face good, telling me how bad I was playing and all that stuff.

At halftime, we got in the locker room and told each other that we hadn't come this far to lose. That we were not going to go back on the plane losers. We had to find a way. I remember Tony Apostle, a halfback from Tacoma, saying, "Six, you've got to say something." But all I said was, "Hey, that's a long plane ride and we don't want to go back losers. Let's get it together."

But it's hard to be positive sometimes when you are down 21-0 at halftime on the road.

We got a big break, however, when Bob Ferguson, a linebacker who is now the general manager for the Seattle Seahawks, picked off a pass, and then we went down and scored. Then we scored again and it was 21-14, and suddenly all the plays were working.

One of the real keys was our base defense. It really stopped a good Purdue team that also included running back Otis Armstrong, who ended up leading the NFL in rushing a few years later.

With 2:04 left, Steve Wiezbowski made a 25-yard field goal, and we went ahead 22-21. We ended up winning by that score. At the time, it was the greatest comeback in school history—it has since been topped by the 1988 team that came back from 27-3 in the third quarter to beat Cal.

As time ran out, I just couldn't wait to run through all those Purdue guys on the way to the locker room. Oh man, was that fun.

A Tough Season

Overall, however, 1972 was kind of a rough season, especially after how well things had gone my sophomore and junior years.

We hosted Oregon in the middle of the season, and I was so sick I couldn't see. Greg Collins came in and had a great game, and we won 23-17 when Calvin Jones knocked away two or three Dan Fouts passes at the end of the game. I remember they went for it on fourth down and Calvin knocked it down, just like he had on third down.

That didn't make any sense to me, to throw at an All-America cornerback with the game on the line.

The next week we were 5-0 and headed to Stanford for a rematch against a team that had beaten us the last two years.

I remember warming up before the game, I felt great. The first part of the game, I felt we were going to really beat them. This Stanford team wasn't quite as good as the ones the two years previous that had gone to the Rose Bowl—they ended up finishing 6-5 that year and only 2-5 in conference play. But I got dragged down from behind on a safety blitz, hurt my knee, and couldn't finish the game. We lost 24-0—the only shutout during my career—and I ended up missing the next three games.

A Controversial Ending

I came back to play one last game in Husky Stadium, and we beat UCLA, a nice way to go out at home. It's probably too bad my career didn't end with that UCLA game.

The next week we had to travel to Spokane to play Washington State, and that was a good Cougar team that ended up finishing No. 20 in the country.

But it was a tough game for us to play. We had beaten them my first two years, and we didn't have much to play for. That was back in the days when only the conference champion got to go to a bowl game. If we had played now, we probably would have gone to three straight bowl games, and definitely my last two years when we spent much of the season ranked in the top 20. And that game against the Cougars probably would have meant something for both of us—WSU went 7-4 that year.

Instead, the week before that WSU game our only real motivation was to win a game against a team we'd beaten twice already. We knew we were going to be 8-3 at worst.

I remember having a weird feeling all week that guys really weren't that motivated. It showed on the field as the Cougars beat us 27-10.

That game is remembered these days mostly for a sack that a Cougar defender named Gary Larsen made on me, which he then celebrated afterward by doing an Indian dance and whooping like you'd see in an old John Wayne movie.

For him to say now that it was just a celebration dance is wrong. Hey, they won the game, so he can do what he wants. But there's no way he'd get away with that today.

It was a tough way to go out. But as far as being a Washington Husky, I wouldn't change a thing.

Chapter 2

THE COACHES

Through the years, Washington coaches have been a big factor in making Washington football as great as it's been.

I wish I could have been around to meet Gil Dobie, who started Washington's great coaching tradition almost 100 years ago when he led the Huskies on a 58-0-3 run from 1908-1916. Some of the old-timers still tell stories of how Dobie was known to be one of the toughest taskmasters of his day, a perfectionist who was rarely satisfied with anything.

One famous story goes that a UW player once ran 90 yards for a touchdown and then came off the field expecting to get some hearty congratulations from his coach.

Instead, Dobie simply told the player, "If you were any good, you would do it more often," and turned away.

I'm not sure that approach would work today, but no one can deny that Dobie began a long line of great Washington coaches. In fact, Dobie's team at one point won 39 straight games, which ranked as the best in college football history until Oklahoma's famous 47-game win streak from 1953-57.

I've been fortunate in my time around the program to get to know and work closely with two of UW's other greats—Jim Owens and Don James.

Here are some thoughts on those two, as well as other coaches I've known at Washington.

The Big Man

That's what we called Jim Owens because he was, simply, a Big Man. He was 6'4" and just towered over most of us.

He was tough, but in my case, I thought he was fair. He pushed us hard, but he worked hard himself and just wanted us to work as hard as he did. Obviously it was a philosophy that worked a lot of the time, given the success he had.

One thing about Jim, he wasn't a "tower guy" like Don James. He was the kind of guy who liked to be a physical and vocal part of practice. It didn't matter who you were, he'd come and get on you.

Some of the guys called him "J.O." as well.

But not to his face. Then we called him "Coach Owens." We weren't that dumb.

Jim Owens

The Big Man Gets Bloody

One of my most vivid memories of J.O. is the day he took Bill Cahill aside during a tackling drill because he didn't like the way it was going. Cahill was one of our best players—he ended up in the NFL with the Buffalo Bills.

But for some reason, this day he thought Billy was screwing around, and he said, "Gosh darn it, Cahill"—or something like that—and called him over.

I was on another side of the field doing another drill, and suddenly I heard this commotion. I looked over and Coach Owens was showing him how to tackle. Coach Owens was getting right up in his face mask—without having a helmet or any protection—and he had cuts on the bridge of his nose and blood is streaming down his face. He was saying, "That's Husky football."

You couldn't do anything but say "yes sir" after you saw something like that.

I mean, he had blood streaming down his face. We didn't want him coming over to where we were looking like that. But that's the way he was. He liked to get right in there.

Teaching Us How

Since he was a former tight end, Coach Owens also liked to demonstrate technique on running pass routes. Every once in a while he would get out there and run one. He ran on the tip of his toes, and we always thought it was kind of funny-looking, though I don't think any of us ever told him that.

Another vivid memory for me is of him coming out and catching warmup passes from me. I tried not to heat them in there too much, but once in a while, I'd get some mustard on it. I used to chuckle to myself seeing him try to catch those. But that's just how hands-on he wanted to be.

The Fumble Drill

One time I found out personally just how involved Jim would get in drills.

I fumbled a snap once, and he was so mad he came running over to me and threw the ball on the ground and told me to jump on it. He didn't think I jumped on it quickly enough, so he knocked it out of my hands and made me do it again and again and again. That taught us that if there was a ball on the ground, you had better get on it. Even in practice.

It's amazed me sometimes when I go to some practices these days. You'll see a guy fumble a snap and it's like it's no big deal. In my day, if there was a ball on the ground during a practice, you'd better get on it.

I think that kind of stuff made a difference when it came to the games.

Riverside

Jim didn't want to waste a lot of time in practice, even if a player was injured.

Usually, if someone got hurt and needed attention, Jim would just yell "Riverside" and we would turn around and run the play the other way.

That became a big joke among all of us players, yelling "Riverside."

The Big Man Gets Emotional

One thing that Jim Owens always liked to do was give you a word of encouragement. Many times he would slap me on the rear end before I went on the field. But you have to understand, the pads back there aren't very thick. You wear those big ones on your hips, but you don't really have anything on your backside. And he would just whack you. It wasn't just a clap; it was a slap.

A few times I would put my hands back there before he wound up so he would slap my hands and not my rear end. It was, "Hey, Jim, take it easy."

But that's how into the game he was. He was always very demonstrative.

I think the most emotional I ever saw him after a game was my sophomore year when we lost at USC in a night game, 28-25. It had been a tight game all the way. We had something like three drives of more than 90 yards and our defense had held them on a fourth and goal inside the five-yard line. And still we lost.

We were so emotionally drained. Afterward in the locker room, he had tears in his eyes talking about how close we had come and how hard we had worked. He said it in such an emotional way. To see your head coach like that, you couldn't help tearing up yourself.

It's always amazed me how your emotions can get so wrapped up in the game. You just get so emotionally stressed. And that was one time that Jim showed it.

Getting Us Ready

Coach Owens could be just as emotional before a game as well.

He never let anybody in the locker room before a game as I guess happens sometimes now. He expected you to get your game face on by yourself. If the game was at 1:30, we knew that at 1:20, here would come the Big Man throwing open the door and giving us that little speech to fire us up.

Then we would say a little prayer on one knee, and after that, it was time to head down the tunnel. The excitement level would just build to the point that we couldn't wait to run down that tunnel and get onto the field. And there was nothing better than hitting that tunnel and hearing the crowd.

He'd really get us fired up. But he wasn't a swearer. He'd just use that Southern Oklahoma drawl that he had. And his speeches really weren't that complicated. They weren't colored with a lot of the flowery stuff you see in the movies. It was mostly, "This is what we have to do today, take care of that football," those kinds of things.

But we were usually ready to play.

Dining with the Big Man

I don't mean to make it sound like playing for Coach Owens wasn't without its fun times. He was tough, but he also let us know that he appreciated us.

He lived right across the lake from Husky Stadium in the Laurelhurst—it was straight across from the flagpole, and we always used to joke that he walked to work.

But he would host these little get-togethers for the players at his house and have these barbecues for us and take care of us in that way. I know there was some controversy about how Coach Owens treated some players, but as far as I saw it, he was always fair with everybody.

I mean, I have to give him a lot of credit for taking a skinny kid out of Ashland, Oregon, and letting him throw the football around. I'll always be proud of that.

The TD Club

It's funny, but in the 1972 UW football media guide, it says that I won the "Touchdown Club of Ohio's Sammy Baugh Trophy" in 1970 "but was unable to attend" the banquet.

I was unable to attend because Coach Owens wouldn't let me go.

I was just 19 years old, and I guess Coach Owens wasn't sure how I'd deal with all the attention of being flown back to Columbus, being waited on by a couple of hosts, dining with a bunch of celebrities, etc. They ended up sending me the prize—which was a helmet lamp that I still have somewhere.

But maybe Coach Owens did the right thing by not letting me get too caught up in things. Because the next year the same club honored me again, and that time Coach Owens let me go. I remember hanging out there with guys like Pat Sullivan, who had just won the Heisman Trophy, and Tommy Casanova and Ed Marinaro and thinking to myself, "What the heck am I doing here? These guys are really good."

That year, though, there was no lamp. Just a plaque.

Here Comes Don

After coach Owens retired in 1974, the Huskies hired Don James to take over.

Nobody in Seattle knew much about Don at the time, however.

There's the famous story about how he was welcomed to town by a banner that said "Welcome, Coach Jones." That's how little anybody out here knew of him.

He came from Kent State, remember, which wasn't exactly known as a hotbed of football, though Don had led the team to some good seasons with a linebacker named Jack Lambert.

And I have to admit that few of us former players knew much about him, either. All I knew was that I was hoping he was the man for the job.

I was playing professionally most of 1973 and 1974, and when I came back, you'd watch those last two teams that Jim had and they were just horrible. They didn't seem like the same Huskies that I had been around.

I guess it was time for a change.

The New Regime

It was kind of odd at first to see a guy come in from what seemed like such a small program at Kent State to take over at a place like Washington. But one thing a lot of people overlooked was that Don had been around guys like Bo Schembechler and had been an assistant at Florida State and Colorado and played at Miami. He had a lot of experience at big-time schools coming in.

When DJ got here, everybody wanted to embrace him.

But one thing about Don, he was a little more distant than Coach Owens was, a little more reserved.

Maybe it's because he had so much work to do.

He was like a Dick Vermeil-type back then, sleeping in his office and all of that.

But then we saw those first teams play with Warren Moon and all those other guys, and it was obvious that things were changing.

James was wired by Joe Kearney, the AD when I played. After Joe decided to move on, Mike Lude took over the athletic department, and one thing that helped Don was that Mike Lude was definitely a football guy.

He was an old coach, and the coach in him never left him. He liked being out at practice and being part of the process. I can still see him out there on the field with his stopwatch, timing punts and snaps and things like that. You'd see him around the team a lot.

But one thing Don did was make the program his own from the very beginning. Unlike some coaches who follow legends, Don never seemed intimidated by his pred-

Don James

ecessor. It probably helped Don that he took over after two of Jim's worst years.

But when Don took over, it was immediately clear that it was his way or no way. I was in Hawaii during most of Don's first season in 1975, but you could tell just by reading the newspaper accounts of what was going on that the program was on an upswing, that there was some athletic ability coming in, and that the future was bright.

The Tower

The one thing everybody really remembers about Don James was his tower. Coach James would watch every practice from a tower that stood about 15 feet above the field. The newspapers use to run pictures of Don's head peering out of this purple tower, with a notepad and pencil in hand, charting everything that was happening on the field.

It was definitely a change from Coach Owens, who as I mentioned liked to be down on the field participating in everything.

I know Don always said that it allowed him to have a better overall view of both the offense and the defense. I think he also felt that it allowed him to take a more disappassionate view of the practices. Players couldn't tell if he was angry at them or not.

Don's way was to notice the mistakes, things he wanted to change, and then tell the assistants. The assistants would then tell the players.

It was definitely different, and I have to admit that a lot of us ex-players—so used to the way Coach Owens would coach, being down on the field and in the middle of the action—thought the way Don did things was a little weird. But he certainly proved us wrong.

The Bus

One of my favorite stories about Don is the time the team was bussing down to a game in Oregon. Don liked everything to go according to plan—he was very meticulous. There was bus one, bus two, bus three, bus four, etc. And they were supposed to head down to Oregon in that order.

Only the driver of bus two decided for some reason to pass bus number one, the bus Don was on. Don was furious, and when they got to Portland, Don made a few calls and had the driver of bus two sent home and replaced by a new driver who, presumably, wasn't going to pass bus number one.

But that's how Don was. Rules were rules with him.

Different Philosophies

Things like the tower make you think about the different way coaches do things and how coaches learn from each other.

When Jim Lambright took over for Don, for instance, he got rid of the tower and got back down on the field. That makes some sense if you think about it, since Jim had played for Coach Owens and began his coaching career under Owens, as well.

Current coach Keith Gilbertson, however, has talked of bringing back the tower. I know there are times he likes to go up high in the stadium and get above it all, the way Don did. That makes some sense, too, considering Keith has always regarded Coach James as one of his biggest influences in coaching. One of Coach Gilbertson's first jobs was working as a graduate assistant for Don James in the mid-70s.

Out with the Old

Don made the program his own in a lot of ways. One of the first, and most noticable, was changing the old uniforms and helmets.

Don likes stripes, so we went to those gold helmets with the stripes and the W on them.

Another tradition that went by the wayside in those days was the alumni game.

We used to end spring practice every year by playing the alumni. Those were valuable practice games and fun as well, as we'd play against all these guys who were playing in the NFL.

It was kind of a reward, really, and no one took it too seriously. Coach Owens always felt like he knew where guys were by that point and the spring game wasn't going to make or break where you stood with the team, although there's no question it helped me in 1970 when I played so well.

But Don felt differently. He and his staff looked at that as a final chance to see the players and have guys competing for jobs. In his eyes, it was make or break for at least a couple of guys each spring and what they needed to do heading into the fall.

One of the last alumni games was in 1976 in the Kingdome, which helped turn me into a trivia answer for a while. I played quarterback for the alumni and ended up throwing the first touchdown pass in the Kingdome—which had just recently opened.

The 1977 spring game was the last one played against the alumni. They thought there was too much of a chance for guys to get hurt, and it was getting harder for NFL guys to come back and play, as well, because their teams were worried guys would get hurt. Obviously, such a game would never be played today because no NFL team would let their players take part.

But at the time, a lot of us felt kind of slighted when they did away with it.

Coming back to play was a great chance to see everybody again and for us to really meet the new players. It took a number of years before they came up with some new ways for a lot of us alums to get back in the program.

The Adaptable Coach

One of the things that made Coach James so great was his ability to adapt and change.

The way the Huskies played when he first took over was much different from the way the team played when he retired. Washington was primarily a running team for years, but by the end of his coaching tenure, the Huskies were running the one-back offense and flinging the ball all over the place.

But I'll admit that when Don first took over, a lot of us questioned his approach to games.

Some guys thought he played it too close to the vest. It seemed a lot of times like he was playing not to lose instead of playing to win. That was different from the way Coach Owens usually did things, which was why a lot of us questioned it at first.

But it soon became clear that Don knew what he was doing, that he was simply playing the percentages.

Don *was* playing not to lose. But it wasn't out of fear. Instead, Don's thinking was that before you could win the game, you had to not lose it. And there's no question that philosophy paid off in a number of big wins through the years.

Getting Aggressive

I don't think it was really until Jim Lambright started with his eight-man defensive front in 1989 that the Huskies really became an aggressive team under coach James.

But Don saw that it was time to change some things and wasn't afraid to do it, and that was one of his greatest strengths. You see all kinds of coaches who last a long time who don't adjust as well as Don did, and sometimes it costs them at the end of their careers.

Don also adjusted his recruiting philosophy along the way.

At first it seemed like he was into bigger players so we could go mano a mano against other teams. But that seemed to become a detriment in the mid-1980s, especially in that Sun Bowl in 1986 against Alabama when Cornelius Bennett just ran around us all day as the Tide crushed us 28-6. Bennett really showed us that speed was the name of the game and that it was time for us to get some more speed.

It didn't take Don long to figure that out and start recruiting athletes with more speed, and that helped pay off in the great teams in the early 1990s.

The other thing about Don was he always had a good staff. That might have been why he was so comfortable coaching from the tower, because he had confidence that his assistants would do the job.

The guys whom Don had around him were amazing—Jim Mora, Gary Pinkel, Skip Hall, Bob Stull—a lot of guys who went on to be head coaches at other places.

Jim Lambright

Jim Lambright's first year as a coach at UW was my first year as a player—1969. Jim had also played under Coach Owens and he had a lot of Jim Owens in him—he was a hard-nosed coach who really got after it.

Jim did a great job as an assistant for all those years and then got the head coaching job in about as tough a circumstance as you can imagine—after Don retired in the wake of the sanctions from the Pac-10 and the NCAA.

I remember talking to Jim once he got the head coaching job, and it was evident that he couldn't wait to get rid of the stripes and get back to the purple helmets and get guys in white shoes—he thought they looked faster in white shoes. He also wanted to get back to more of a plain Jane traditional look, more of a workmanlike uniform.

It didn't necessarily go over all that well with players and fans, who associated the stripes and gold helmets with all of the success of Don's era.

There's no question that one of Jim's biggest problems was that he was never really in step with athletic director

Barbara Hedges. I always believed that a head football coach and the AD should be hooked in arms—otherwise, you have nothing more than division within the company. I think that's what we had there for a few years and that hurt Jim and it hurt the football program.

Lambright's Whammy

I thought Jim might be okay after the famous Whammy in Miami game when we beat the Hurricanes in the Orange Bowl to end their 58-game home winning streak.

I mean, he did a great job of keeping that team together after all the turmoil associated with Don stepping down, and when they won that game, I really thought it might be rosy forever for Jim.

But then there were some bad situations that hurt Jim, like the 1994 loss at Oregon when Kenny Wheaton made that interception after we didn't get the ball to Napoleon Kaufman at the end of the game.

There was also the deal with Shane Fortney, the quarterback from Everett who I thought was one of the best athletes I've ever seen. Shane could do so many things.

But he got hurt in a game early in the 1996 season, and Jim left him in there. I remember at the time wondering why he was still in the game. Shane ended up leaving the next year, and I'm not sure Jim handled that real well. There were a lot of situations like that that led to Jim's downfall.

Still, I think Jim should be remembered for all the good things he did at UW. He was player, assistant coach and head coach there and wore purple about as long as anybody in school history. That shouldn't be forgotten.

Rick Neuheisel

Rick's time at Washington ended a little ugly to say the least. But his time at UW is a part of our history, good or bad. I have to admit that I was as shocked as anyone when they hired him in 1999 to replace Jim Lambright. Usually when you get to a big program like this you've been a head coach for some time, even if it's at another level. But Rick had been head coach at Colorado for just four years, and all of his other experience was at UCLA. Even at the time they hired him I remember wondering how he was going to fit in.

When Rick got here, I also thought he brought in a lot of guys who didn't really understand Husky football.

Don James had also been new when he came in, but he had had a lot of experience at a lot of different places. I also thought he took the time to understand what Husky football was all about, which I think played a big part in his succes.

Rick had a lot of success his first two years, but I think he inherited a lot of quality kids. That 2000 team was a very strong senior team with that offensive line and Marques Tuiasosopo.

To the Future

Keith Gilbertson took over in a tough spot following Neuheisel's firing. I remember shortly after he got the job he told me that it would take two years to get the program back to where it needs to be. As I write this in the spring of 2004, I think the program is making great strides and that we are heading in the right direction.

Watching the Huskies now reminds me a little bit of being in Chuck Knox's camp with the Rams in 1973. Chuck used to say, "We are going to be tougher, smarter, and in better condition." I think that's what the Huskies are doing, getting back to Husky football and back to where we were when the program was so successful.

Chapter 3

THE QUARTERBACKS

One of the things I'm proudest of is being part of the great line of Washington quarterbacks.

Did you know that since 1975, every Washington starting quarterback has played professionally?

It's a staggering list, beginning with Warren Moon and ending—as this was written—with Marques Tuiasosopo—each two of the greatest QBs not only in Washington history but in college football history. (As this was written, Cody Pickett's NFL future had yet to be determined.)

It's no coincidence that the streak began with the arrival of Don James.

Don always had good quarterbacks coaches, and he had a good eye for recruiting quarterbacks. He usually went for athletic types who could run as well as throw, and that always allowed us to be versatile offensively.

Don also usually made his QBs sit for a while as he groomed them to become starters. A few guys started as sophomores, but I think Warren Moon is the only QB Don ever had who started his first year in the program. Everybody else had to sit and watch for a few years, which meant they not only got acclimated to the system, but got bigger, stronger and more confident in what they were doing. By the time their number was called, they were ready to go.

That makes a big difference. College football is littered with QBs who were rushed to play too early and ran into problems. But at Washington, almost no quarterback has ever had to play before he was ready, and I think that's one reason so many of them have been so successful.

Here are some of my thoughts on the quarterbacks I have seen and known in my time at Washington.

Denny Fitzpatrick

Denny Fitzpatrick was on the team with me for a couple of years, and then he followed me and started some games after I left.

He still holds one of the more interesting records in UW history, rushing for 249 yards against Washington State in 1974. That's the most rushing yards for any QB not only in UW history but in Pac-10 history as well. In fact, it's still the fifth most rushing yards any UW player has had in one game.

Denny got those yards running the option offense— pretty much the same offense Owens wanted to run when I got there before we thankfully switched to more of a passing attack once I got the job.

Denny's had a good post-football career, as he's now working as the general manager of the Beverly Hilton Hotel in Beverly Hills, the famous hotel owned by Merv Griffin. The Huskies have stayed there a few times through the years.

One of my favorite stories about Denny, however, involves the USC game in 1972 when I was out with an injury.

That was that great USC team that some say is among the best in the history of college football. I was trying to keep him loose before the game, and I said, "Hey Denny, just be yourself. All they do is hit hard." But I was thinking afterward that that might have been the wrong thing to say. I think I might have made him a little more nervous.

Denny did get hit hard a few times, and we lost 34-7, although it wouldn't have mattered who the QB was that day. USC went undefeated and won the national title that year.

Warren Moon

Few quarterbacks have had a bigger impact on the Washington program than Warren Moon.

He was Don James's first big recruit. He had played at a junior college in Los Angeles for a year before coming up here, so nobody here knew much about him.

The fact that he was black also was noteworthy at the time. Washington had never had a black quarterback, and there weren't that many in college football at the time. It's

Warren Moon

just a fact that a lot of people wondered how this was all going to work out. And it wasn't that far removed from the black player revolt, which had happened   just six years earlier.

You really have to give a lot of credit to Don James for that. He made a big statement that it didn't matter if you were green, purple, black or blue—if you could play, he would play you. To make such a statement so early in his coaching career really meant something.

I was still in Hawaii playing early in that season, so I didn't know much about Warren until I got back for that come-from-behind win in the '75 Apple Cup.

You could tell just by watching practice that he was the real deal. He was 6'3", had a strong arm, and was a good athlete. I remember, too, that he had such good mechanics at the time—the way he moved his feet and squared his shoulders. That led me to believe that the year he had at the JC really helped his skills, because he seemed to come here ready to play.

That doesn't mean he didn't have a lot to learn, however.

A lot of people's most vivid memory of Warren early in his career was the game against Cal that we lost 7-0. We were driving late in the game, and on a fourth-down play, Warren threw the ball out of bounds and that was that.

But he was a young QB and he just got caught up in the game. That was just inexperience. But I think that might also have been the moment when Don first started thinking that maybe he needed to bring his QBs along a little more slowly before they started playing in games.

Warren got progressively better, however, and his performance in 1977 was, obviously, one of the biggest reasons the Huskies won the Rose Bowl that year.

Tom Porras

Tom Porras may be one of the more forgotten QBs in Washington history. He sat behind Warren most of his career before getting a chance to start in 1978. We went 7-4 that year, actually the same record as the year before when we went to the Rose Bowl, but we lost the wrong games in Pac-10 play and ended up not gong to any bowl game at all. For a long time, that was the last season in which we didn't go to a bowl game under Don James, which may be one reason Tom seems like a forgotten man at times.

It's kind of funny but when I think of Tom, I remember mostly that he was a musician. They called him the "singing quarterback" because he liked his music—he liked singing ballads if I remember right.

Unlike most of the rest of the guys on this list, Tom never played in the NFL, but he did see some action for a few years in the USFL.

Tom Flick

Tom was one of the first of a long line of in-state star quarterbacks to become the starter for the Huskies.

In fact, he attended Interlake High in Bellevue, just like Steve Pelluer, who followed him as the starter in high school and college.

Tom might have been the most graceful quarterback I've ever seen play for us. He just had a nice air about him, the way he dropped back, the way he threw the ball.

He always seemed under control. Maybe that was just part of his makeup—I think of the fact that he later became a motivational speaker. That makes a lot of sense because I remember that he was always just so positive.

That had to rub off when he led us to the Rose Bowl in 1980 with a team that really was pretty young and had to bounce back from a brutal loss early in the season to Oregon in our first conference game. But we then won seven in a row, including an upset of No. 2 USC, to win the Pac-10 title.

Tom didn't have the strongest arm in the world, but he was very accurate—he had great anticipation throwing the football. There was one game against Arizona when he completed 16-17 passes, still the best completion percentage for a game in UW history.

It makes sense that he still holds the school record for career completion percentage. He completed 60.3 percent of his passes and was better than 60 percent every year he played.

Steve Pelluer

Steve was the next in that line of in-state QBs to become a starter for us.

He was a big kid who could also scramble a bit. He probably had a stronger arm than Tom Flick, and he really threw the long ball well.

He had a number of memorable games, like the day he completed 19-25 passes at UCLA in a shootout with a Bruin quarterback named Rick Neuheisel.

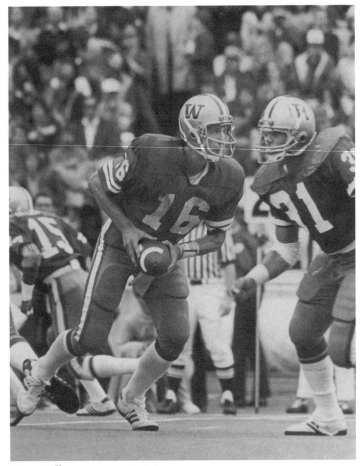

Steve Pelluer

He was also the starting QB for the 1982 Rose Bowl, which the Huskies won 28-0 over Iowa.

But the game of Steve's that really stands out for me came against Michigan in 1983. We were down 24-10 after Michigan scored early in the fourth quarter, and I think most people thought the game was over.

But then Steve led two scoring drives, including throwing a TD pass and a two-point conversion with 34 seconds left to win the game. I remember on that last drive it just seemed like every pass was a completion. He was 27-33 that day in what I still think is one of the greatest performances by a UW QB I've seen.

What I also remember about Steve is meeting him at Don James's house before he was even a Husky. It was an event where they brought all the blue-chip recruits in, and I just remember how well Steve handled himself. It's easy for kids in that situation—quarterbacks who are being courted by a lot of schools—to come off like they are full of themselves.

But it was typical of the QBs that Don recruited that they always seemed like good character kids as well as good athletes, like the coaches had really done their homework. I think that was why so many of them were so successful. Steve certainly epitomized that in my mind.

Tim Cowan

One thing Steve had to do for a couple of years—and that became common for a while under Don—was share time with Tim Cowan.

Tim was a guy who really worked hard to get where he was.

He was from Cerritos, California, and when I first saw him, I'll admit I didn't think much of him. He just didn't seem that physically impressive.

Maybe one of the reasons was his style. Every quarterback has a different style. In that era, I remember that Flick was more of a slinger; Pelluer threw more overhand. But Tim Cowan really threw with an overhand delivery. It looked kind of odd, but the ball would get there.

And the more he played, the more he kept making plays. That's probably what Don thought, as well, as Tim ended up starting two games in 1981 and four in 1982 when Steve was struggling.

Tim capped his time at Washington with one of the best performances in a bowl game I've ever seen, that 1982 Aloha Bowl against Maryland when he completed 33 of 53 passes for 350 yards, no interceptions and three touchdowns. The last TD came with six seconds left and won the game.

It's hard to find an individual performance much better in Husky history, and Tim really outdueled the other QB on the field that day—a guy for Maryland named Boomer Esiason (Boomer completed 19 of 32 passes for 251 yards).

One thing I will say is that Tim and Steve Pelluer each benefited greatly from having Anthony Allen as one of their receivers. Allen had eight catches for 152 yards in that Aloha Bowl and caught all three touchdowns—one of the greatest receiving games I've ever seen a Husky have as well. He was really unbelievable and definitely one of my favorite UW receivers.

Hugh Millen

Hugh was a Seattle guy who always wanted to be a Husky.

I remember going down to Roosevelt High School, where he played, and playing basketball with Hugh when he was in high school. But I remember he didn't seem that tall.

Then all the sudden I read about Hugh Millen signing with the Huskies to play QB and he's 6'5". How did that happen? I think he's still the tallest QB we've had.

The one thing about Hugh was he was a real student of the game. He really studied film and worked at getting better, and it seems fitting that he's now a football analyst in Seattle, working on TV and radio. He always had that kind of mind.

Hugh's competition for the starting job when he played in 1984 was Paul Sicuro. Like me, Paul was from Ashland, Oregon, so even though I always wanted them both to do well, I always kind of rooted for Paul.

That was another era when Don James would really use two quarterbacks.

In 1984, Hugh started nine games and Paul Sicuro started three.

Sicuro started the Orange Bowl that year against Oklahoma. But when he struggled, Hugh came off the bench and helped win the game.

That's the luxury of having two quarterbacks, if you can make it work by massaging the egos of the players involved. Even when I played we did that a few times. There were games where I wasn't right at the start and Greg

Collins would come in for a series or two. That would settle me down and then I'd go back in.

I don't know why coaches don't do that any more. There's no question Don did that a lot more than anybody else does now, which is another way that Don was ahead of the game.

It's funny because that 1984 team was one of the best in school history—it went 11-1 and finished No. 2 in the country. Yet you rarely heard about the QBs back then because that defense was so good with Tim Meamber, Ron Holmes, Jimmy Rodgers, Reggie Rogers, etc.

Those guys got all the headlines, which is kind of different for such a good team to seem to have two QBs who were relatively under the radar. But when you had those guys playing such good defense, who wouldn't write about them more?

Chris Chandler

I really loved him. He was from Everett, a tough local kid who went to the same high school that Jim Lambright did and seemed to have the same kind of old-school attitude.

You could tell he would be successful because everybody really liked to follow him. A lot of coaches say that's a key in being a successful quarterback, that you have to be the guy on the team who everybody else wants to be around. Chris Chandler was definitely that type of guy.

He was also a great athlete, as good as any QB who has ever played for us. He could play basketball, golf, any-

Chris Chandler

thing he wanted. He was one of those guys who was so good at everything that you'd be jealous—can't I beat him at something? He was kind of like a John Elway-type in talent, which has been proven in the long NFL career he had after leaving UW. As I wrote this in 2004, Chris Chandler was still the only UW alum to start a Super Bowl at quarterback, leading Atlanta there in 1998 to play Denver.

Plus, he just looked like a quarterback. He had a square jaw and always had a day's growth of beard going.

We didn't win any Rose Bowls with Chris as quarterback because there were some other areas of the team that were struggling a little bit then. But of all the QBs we've had, he would be right there on my list of favorites.

Cary Conklin

One of the things I really remember about Cary is how we didn't really think we'd get him at first. He grew up in Yakima and everybody seemed to think he'd be going to Washington State.

But that was another example of how Don James really made recruiting in-state a big priority. His whole philosophy was to recruit the state first, then go out of state. I don't think he missed on more than one or two of the top in-state QBs because of that. Maybe Drew Bledsoe or Mark Rypien, who each went to Washington State, though they were both from the other side of the state to begin with.

Getting Cary was a big coup at the time. He was a huge guy, but he wasn't quite the scrambler that some of the others were. But he could really throw. He set a bunch of records in 1989 that weren't broken until the last few years.

Cary also has always been one of my favorite persons to play QB. He's just a great guy.

Billy Joe Hobert

My first memory of Billy Joe Hobert is seeing him play for Puyallup in the high school state title game on a bad ankle. I knew then he was coming to Washington, and I thought, "Man, we're getting a tough kid here."

We had all heard the stories then about him being a street kid from Tacoma and what a great athlete he was, but then when I watched that game, I really realized he was a player.

I always loved his moxie. He just wanted to play football. Let's go play—that's the attitude he had on and off the field. Maybe some guys didn't like that about him— the swagger he had, the way he carried himself—but that was Billy Joe.

And he had the perfect name. The way he played, the way he acted, he couldn't have been named Michael or something. But Billy Joe seemed to fit.

It's too bad now that he's remembered mostly for the way his career ended. Because when he played, he was one of the greatest in UW history. The Huskies were 17-0 in games he started and 27-0 in games in which he played—a record that obviously can never be topped.

He also threw 27 touchdowns compared to just 13 interceptions—the best touchdown-to-interception ratio of any of the great UW quarterbacks—and was MVP of the 1992 Rose Bowl, the game that clinched the national title.

And you have to remember he had attempted only six passes before he became the starter in 1991 when Mark Brunell was hurt in spring practice. I'm not sure any UW QB has ever done better with so little experience. Certainly, he had a lot to work with that year, but talk to UW coaches and they'll tell you that not just any QB could have handled that situation as well as Billy Joe did.

As for how he got in trouble? You have to remember how young these guys are. It sounds like a cop-out at times, but it's easy to get caught up in all of that when you are that young. And he just had that swagger—maybe he had it too much and it caught up to him a little bit.

I've always thought they should change that rule, anyway, and allow college athletes to get loans based on their future earnings. That's what a regular student does, doesn't he, if he takes out a loan to go to law school? It makes no sense.

But I can't fault Billy Joe for what he did as a Husky. I admired him as a player.

Mark Brunell

Mark had a great UW career and an even better one in the NFL.

But think how great it might have been if he hadn't gotten hurt and missed much of that 1991 season.

He was really the first true QB that Don James brought in who was left-handed.

That might not sound like a big deal, but there are a lot of adjustments a team has to make for a left-handed quarterback. Think about it, if you put your best tackle at left tackle to protect a QB's blind side, he's got to go to the right side if your QB is left-handed. Many offenses are made for the right side to be the strong side of the formation. But if your QB is left-handed, you have to change it. Mark Brunell was worth it to make those adjustments.

When I think of Mark, I actually remember a game he played in that he lost more than any of the wins. Specifically, the 1992 Apple Cup, the dreaded Snow Bowl loss to Washington State in Pullman.

The Cougars blew us out in the third quarter, taking a big lead. But here was Mark, a senior quarterback, taking us down the field to get more points on the board late in the game. He could have gone in the tank that day if he wanted to, but he didn't—he led us to two touchdowns in the last five minutes of the game.

To me, that says a lot about the guy.

Then there was the 1990 game at Colorado, the 20-14 loss that helped cost us a chance at the national title. He led us on a drive late in the game and threw three passes right at the end that should have been caught for touchdowns.

He was also interesting because he was such a contrast from Billy Joe on and off the field. He didn't have that swagger—he led in a completely different way.

But in his own way, he was just as effective.

Damon Huard

Damon had one of the more star-crossed careers of any Husky QB.

He arrived in 1991 when we won the national title, and at the time we were really going after guys from proven systems, guys who already played the game. Obviously, he had played for his father, just like Billy Joe and his brothers did as well, and that was a great proving ground for them and a great pipeline for us.

Damon didn't have the strongest arm in the world, and he wasn't the greatest athlete. He wasn't really the classic pocket passer, either. With his arm level, delivery and speed, he looked a little methodical to me at times.

But he had a tremendous competitive spirit.

The game I remember Damon most for is the 1993 comeback at Cal when we were down 23-3 in the third quarter and he was playing terribly—he threw four interceptions in the game—and then led us back to a win by throwing two touchdown passes in the final 2:06.

I have talked to many people who saw that comeback on their TV in their hotel rooms because they left early.

Unfortunately for Damon, I think a lot of people only remember the 1994 game at Oregon when he threw the interception that Kenny Wheaton returned for a touchdown. But Damon had a lot of other good games in his career, like the Whammy in Miami just a few weeks before the Wheaton deal.

But that Oregon game is a hard one to forget.

I know they still show it every time you go to Eugene. You'd think even they would get tired of it one of these days.

Brock Huard

If ever a guy looked like a quarterback, it was Brock Huard. Big, strong arm. Boy could he throw.

People used to talk all the time about his motion, that he threw off his back foot. I'm not sure that mattered all that much. He didn't have to do what a lot of us did to throw the ball. His arm was so strong, he could just cock his arm and throw.

But for all of his natural talent, the Huskies didn't win as much under Brock as people thought they might. The teams weren't great a couple of those years; Brock got hurt a little bit, and I'm not sure we ever really saw Brock play to his full potential.

But he's still one of the nicest guys ever to play at Washington.

He never seemed to get upset or fiery, which was one thing that people remarked on a lot. I never really sensed that in Brock, either. I just never really saw that fire in Brock that you see in some other QBs.

Marques Tuiasosopo

I don't think there's a player I can remember who has single-handedly brought a team to a new height the way Marques did.

And I'm talking the whole team—offense, defense, kicking game, coaches.

You look at all of our other Rose Bowl teams—there were usually a lot of defensive stars or a great kicking game. But here was a guy that you knew if you could just hold the other team a little bit, you had a chance. I looked it up, and in 2000, our opponents scored 246 points for the season. From 1990-92, when we won three straight Pac-10 titles, our opponents never scored more than 150 points in a season. In fact, none of the other Rose Bowl teams under Don James ever had more than 175 points scored on them.

That shows the pressure Marques was under a lot of times to lead the Huskies to points, yet he always came through.

He just had that magic.

He also played with a zest and a fun that you just don't see all that often, which may be why the rest of the players played so hard for him.

I remember a play once where Marques was going through a hole on an option. He went through it and got hit, and yet you could see a smile on Marques's face as he was doing it, like is there anything better in the world than this? That was Marques.

It goes back to the first time Marques really got to play, leading us to a couple of TDs to keep it close against Nebraska in 1997 when Brock Huard got hurt. Everybody else was in fear, thinking Marques would get beat up and

Marques Tuiasosopo

the game would turn into a huge rout. But here came Marques, like a little puppy, just so excited to be on the field. I still chuckle about that when I see him run on the field.

The other thing about Marques was that he was not afraid to make a play. He was willing to make the play because he had confidence in himself. If you have that confidence and aren't afraid to try to make the play, good things can happen. Some bad things can happen, too, which is why sometimes Marques made a few turnovers here and there. But in Marques's case, more good things happened.

I think one of the best examples of that was a play he made against Oregon State in 1999. He was running an option and he looked like he was about to lose five yards. At the last minute, he pitched the ball to Willie Hurst, who had to grab it out of the air with one hand. Willie then ran 45 yards for a touchdown. If Marques didn't have the confidence in his ability to make a play, he simply would have lost five yards there instead of getting us a touchdown.

But that was Marques.

Cody Pickett

Of all the Husky quarterbacks I've been around, he's probably the one I feel like I knew the least. He was a hard guy to get to know. He was probably the least willing to share himself.

Maybe it's because he spent much of his youth in rodeo, which is more of an individual sport where you just worry about yourself. He just kind of seemed to be his own guy. Not that there is anything wrong with that. That was just his way.

But what a spectacular career he had. The numbers he put up may never be topped by any Husky QB, in part because no team may ever throw as much—who wouldn't throw all the time with Reggie Williams as a receiver?

Unfortunately, he had to follow Marques, who had a sensational career and an ability to make the plays that always needed to be made.

Chapter 4

THE BIG GAMES

Apple Cup 1975 (Washington 28, Washington State 27)

I was in Hawaii for much of the 1975 season, finishing out my career in the WFL. I remember trying to keep track of everything that was going on. It was Don James's first year as coach, and the scores were here and there—a big win over Stanford but a huge loss at Alabama, for instance.

But I remember telling my wife that I wanted to get home in time to see the Apple Cup.

I wasn't sure that was the right decision, as we were sitting there in the stands in the cold and the rain. It was horrible weather, and that kept a lot of people away. The attendance was listed as 57,100, but there weren't anywhere near that many people. People who have only been going to games since the 1980s wouldn't believe how small the crowd was.

I can still see today in my mind Warren Moon and Spider Gaines warming up on the sidelines. This was before Al Burleson made that pickoff to get the Huskies back in the game. Warren threw these passes to Spider, and they were all hitting him in the face mask, bouncing away. I told my wife, "I don't think it's going to happen today."

Then the Cougars were driving and Al Burleson picked off that pass and ran it back 93 yards for a touchdown. It didn't seem possible. Remember, the Cougars were ahead 27-14 with just over three minutes left and had the ball at our 14-yard line. All they really needed was a field goal to put the game away. The story goes that the Cougar coaches wanted to keep the ball on the ground but finally gave in to the players, who wanted to get one more touchdown and really rub it in.

I think this was before the term "Couging it" came up, though maybe this game was the beginning.

Anyway, Al Burleson ran it back for 27-21. Then our defense got revved up and stopped them and we got the ball again.

Then Warren threw that long pass down the middle that got tipped around, and Spider finally ended up with it and ran in for the touchdown to win the game. I think the Cougars have always claimed that the extra point was no good and that the game should have at least ended in a tie.

No matter what, that was the most amazing comeback I've ever seen. Spider's catch was like that Immaculate Reception that Franco Harris made a few years before that.

As big as the comeback was, however, what I think it did for that team was bigger. There were a lot of young guys on that team in Don's first year—Moon, Gaines, Blair Bush, etc.—and getting a win like that to end the year had to be a great way to go into the off season. Plus, we had beaten USC the week before that, and beating the Cougars made it four wins in our last five games.

Rose Bowl 1978 (UW 27, Michigan 20)

That was such a fun time, because we hadn't really expected to be in the Rose Bowl that year—that team started off 1-3—and then we weren't expected to win the game.

One of my fondest memories of that week is being in the lobby of the team hotel with some friends, including Greg Collins, and suddenly Bob Hope walks in. But for some reason, I thought it was Jack Benny. So I'm yelling at him "Jack, hey Jack." Finally, Greg says, "Sonny, that's Bob Hope."

I'll never forget the look on Bob Hope's face—like what are you talking about? But he came over and signed something for my wife—I think he wrote Bob Jack Hope on it.

Anyway, that game was incredible. Michigan was a big favorite, but we took a 24-0 lead. We were playing real loose and aggressive and just dominated the first half. I don't think Michigan was prepared for us to be as good as we were.

That was also back in the day when the thinking was that the Pac-10 was faster than the Big Ten teams, especially on the grass field at the Rose Bowl, and our speed might have surprised them.

But then Michigan came roaring back with Rick Leach throwing all over the place. Who would have figured that going into that game, that we would be the ones running the ball and they would be the ones throwing it?

They were still throwing it at the end of the game when Michael Jackson made that interception near the goal line.

It was such a great setting at the end, with the sun going down behind the mountains and Michael Jackson picking off that pass in the darkness.

Oregon 1979 (Washington 21, Oregon 17)

Okay, so I could probably list just about any win over Oregon given how intense that rivalry has become.

But I've always tried to have fun with it. You have to remember I grew up down there. We always go down to the Oregon games and have fun tailgating.

That was one of those Willamette fall days—it was September 22—where it was foggy and cool and kind of damp in the morning, and then once we got to the game it was 90 degrees and everybody was trying to cut off their jeans. I remember my wife cut the sleeves off of her shirt because it was so hot.

We got behind 17-0, which wasn't much fun because we were sitting in the Oregon section. It wasn't like it is today down there where it's standing room only. Then, there was lots of room.

But we were in the Oregon section because that's where our friends had gotten tickets, and I obviously stood out like a sore thumb. A lot of people were really in my face about how the Ducks were beating us.

And then we started to come back and with just under two minutes to go, our defense held them and they had to punt.

Mark Lee was back to return the kick, and he got the ball at our own 47-yard line. He went 10 or 20 yards and then he reversed his field, and I remember thinking, "What are you doing?" And then all of a sudden he got to the corner and was just gone.

I remember standing up signaling touchdown and somebody threw a piña colada at me. I was sticky as heck going back to the house, but I didn't care. That gave us a 21-17 win and kicked off a memorable year of punt returning for Mark Lee. He returned three for touchdowns that season to set a school record.

I still run into Mark every once in a while, and I always tell him how much joy that punt return brought me down there in Autzen Stadium.

USC 1981 (Washington 13, USC 3)

What a crazy day that was.

To set the stage, we had lost at UCLA the week before, 31-0, and there was a lot of thought that our season was done. USC was ranked No. 3 in the country and had Marcus Allen, who was on his way to winning the Heisman Trophy.

All the Trojans needed to do was beat us to all but wrap up the Pac-10 title.

But all of that was overshadowed by the weather.

That was the wildest day I have ever seen at Husky Stadium with the rain and the wind coming off the lake. You saw papers flying all around the stadium, swirling in the wind. It was so bad, I think even the seagulls stayed home.

Of course, the greatest thing was it was USC in town. Playing in that kind of weather is tough if you're on the road. But when you are at home you are in your element. For us, the weather's always kind of been our secret weapon, especially against the California schools, and it really was that day.

Late in the game, it was a 3-3 tie. Then Chuck Nelson made a 46-yard field goal. To this day, I can't figure out how he could have done that in that weather.

When you talk to kickers, they always say they want to get the right line and then let it go, like a golfer. Chuck's a good golfer too, so that must be how he made that kick that day.

Then on the kickoff, USC couldn't cover it and Fred Small jumped on it in the end zone for a touchdown.

A week later we beat Washington State and were in the Rose Bowl for the second straight year.

Michigan 1983 (Washington 25, Michigan 24)

This one is special for me not only because of the great comeback—we were down 24-10 in the fourth quarter before rallying—but also because of Steve Pelluer's performance.

He was so great on that final drive—I think he was 8-8. I know he didn't miss a pass. And when it's Michigan that you are doing it against—they were ranked No. 8 coming into the game—that's really special.

We were behind all day and really hadn't done much until that fourth quarter. Michigan had pretty much dominated, and I'm sure they felt they were in complete control.

We scored with 9:06 left to make it 24-17 on a TD run by Walt Hunt. But I'm sure Michigan still thought it had the game.

We got the ball back deep in our territory a few minutes later, and it was just like a quarterback clinic the way Steve led us down the field. He threw a seven-yard TD pass to Mark Pattison with 34 seconds left.

Then came the big decision—do we go for the tie or the win?

I've always been a believer in going for the win. I don't think any player wants to tie if there's a way to win the game. I remember thinking, though, because Don James could be kind of conservative at times that he was going to just kick it and take the tie, since it had been such a great comeback already.

Instead, he went for the two, and Pelluer hit tight end Larry Michael for the winning points.

In terms of drama and a QB leading his team down the field at the end of the game, that win is hard to beat.

Orange Bowl 1985 (Washington 28, Oklahoma 17)

This might have been the game that completely cemented Don James's reputation as a great bowl game coach.

We were 10-1 going into the game, but it still seemed like everyone expected Oklahoma to win.

They had players like Brian Bosworth and Tony Casillas, and Barry Switzer running around on the sideline.

Everyone remembers this game for the Sooner Schooner coming onto the field and costing Oklahoma a field goal. Oklahoma had gone ahead 17-14 on a field goal by Tim Lasher when the Schooner raced onto the field in celebration. But the Schooner driver hadn't seen that Oklahoma had been flagged for a penalty, nullifying the field goal. The refs then threw a flag on the Schooner for unsportsmanlike conduct, meaning Oklahoma had to go back 20 yards. Lasher's next kick, which was now a 42-yarder, was blocked, and that seemed to turn the momentum of the game our way.

This was also one of those games where Don James showed he wasn't afraid to use two quarterbacks when necessary. Paul Sicuro started, but he threw three interceptions and Hugh Millen then came in to lead us to two fourth-quarter touchdowns.

Jacque Robinson also had a great game, rushing for 135 yards and becoming the only player ever to be named MVP of the Rose and Orange bowls.

But I think a forgotten key to the game was the running of Rick Fenney. He had nine carries for 66 yards, and it seemed like they all came on trap plays that really got Oklahoma off balance. It wasn't just the yards, but the timing of those trap plays.

I've always felt those trap plays really opened up the rest of the offense for the passing and for Jacque's running, and that was just another great coaching job by Don and his staff to come up with that little wrinkle.

USC 1985 (Washington 20, USC 17)

This game didn't really hold the significance of some of the others on this list, maybe. That was kind of a rebuilding year for us. We finished 7-5 and were never ranked after the first week of the season.

But it was just a fantastic game and the coming-out party for Chris Chandler.

He was a sophomore that year, and he led us on a long drive late in the game, throwing for the winning touchdown to Lonzell Hill with just 56 seconds left.

Every pass Chris had to make on that drive, he made. It wasn't a bunch of long gains, but a lot of little ones. Third and eights, we'd get the first down.

There was a critical fourth and nine where he threw for the first down.

There had been so much hype about Chris. To see him put it all together like that for the first time was really fun.

Freedom Bowl 1989 (Washington 34, Florida 7)

This was a season you could start to see things changing.

We'd had a few down years, by Washington standards, and Don had shaken things up a little bit, and by the end of 1989, you could see it start to come together.

Going into the Freedom Bowl, all you heard about was Emmitt Smith and what a great running back he was. This was his last college game and there was all the hype about what a big-time NFL prospect he was.

And then our defense just shut him down like a fourth-string player. He had just 17 yards on seven carries, which had to be one of the worst days of his career.

I can still see him coming off the field when it was 27-7 and coming over to the sidelines and taking off his shoulder pads and throwing them down and sitting on them. I've never seen a player do that before. It was like he was being a big baby, like he was saying he was taking his ball and going home, like little kids do. It was like he totally gave up.

I could never pull for him after that, even though he did all those great things in the NFL.

There wasn't much drama about the game because we dominated, and it was nice to see some good seniors like Cary Conklin and Andre Riley have big games.

But that was a real stepping-stone game to what happened the next three seasons.

USC 1990 (Washington 31, USC 0)

Everybody remembers this game for Todd Marinovich and his "All I saw was purple" quote afterward.

And that's all he did see, I'm sure. I still can see Steve Emtman and Donald Jones and Dave Hoffman and James Clifford just tearing them up all day.

One of the interesting things about that game was we hadn't really played that well in the first two games of the season. We struggled to beat San Jose State and Purdue and we were ranked just No. 21, while USC was No. 5, largely because of Marinovich, who was thought to be a big star.

But we just dominated from the start, and I remember Marinovich standing on the sideline with his Trojan hood over his head like he was some prima donna.

It was funny because I had met Todd Marinovich when he was just a little kid. His dad, Marv, was a coach for a little while for the WFL team in Hawaii that I played for. Even then, Marv was really into all that health food stuff that became famous once Todd got to USC. We thought he was a little out there, and I never wanted to do anything with my kids like what he did with Todd. You've got to let them be kids.

Todd certainly didn't have any fun that day, though the Huskies did. That game was really the start of our three-year run of dominance in the Pac-10.

Nebraska 1991 (Washington 36, Nebraska 21)

This was one of the biggest wins for the program that I've ever seen.

Everybody knew that the 1991 team was going to be a national title contender—we were in the top five in the preseason in all the major polls. But this was the win that ensured it, that erased all doubt as to UW's worthiness for the national title.

Nebraska was then ranked No. 9 in the country, with coach Tom Osborne and all that went along with that. They simply never lost at home back then.

The big question mark heading into that game was how Billy Joe Hobert would hold up. This was only his second start at QB for us, and it was obvious he would have to play big for us to have a chance.

Billy Joe did just that. In memory, it's easy to think we dominated this game from the start. We won by 15 points, outgained Nebraska 618-308, held the ball for more than 35 minutes, had 31 first downs to their 15, etc.

But Nebraska actually led 21-9 midway through the third quarter. On the next drive, we faced a fourth down near midfield, and Don James decided we had to go for it. Billy Joe hit Orlando McKay for the first down, and that led to a Hobert-to-McKay touchdown pass a few seconds later. We then scored three more TDs in the fourth quarter, scoring the last 27 points of the game.

That was the game that I think really turned Billy Joe into a leader on that team.

One of the amazing things about playing at Nebraska is their fans. They are known for their love and respect for good football, and when the game was over, they gave a standing ovation to our players and coaches as they left the field.

We went back there in 1998, and the Nebraska fans were still appreciative. Though that time, it might have been because they beat us 55-7. Oh well, we'll always have the memory of that 1991 game.

Miami 1994 (Washington 38, Miami 20)

I remember there was so much hype about this game. UW and Miami had shared the national title in 1991, but we felt like we were the real national champs and wanted a chance to prove it. And Miami had won 58 straight games at home, the longest home winning streak in college football history.

But we weren't really playing that great heading into this game, having lost our opener at USC.

I remember that it was one of my first games doing the color analysis for the Husky replays.

The big thing that day was how the players held up in the humidity.

No matter how hard you try, that is just something you cannot prepare for. I remember leaving the hotel the day of the game and getting soaked in sweat just taking my bags out to the bus. I was thinking that if this is happening to me, how are these kids going to play in this weather? That was around the time that those Cool Zones fans started to become a big deal, though, and they needed them that day.

Miami played well early and looked like they might actually really be 14 points better, the way the oddsmakers had called it.

But I'll never forget just before halftime, their QB was trying to get them to go down the sidelines and he threw a pass that fell incomplete and time ran out. Dennis Erickson, their coach, went out and argued that there should still be time left on the clock. I can still see him kicking the pylons as the teams were going off the field. I remember saying on the air that I thought this team might lose its cool after that because they were heading into the locker room acting like they were getting screwed and no one was helping them out. I thought that was a good omen for us.

We dominated the last 30 minutes. There was Richie Chambers picking off a pass, Richard Thomas taking that screen pass into the end zone with a helpful block from Napoleon Kaufman, Bob Sapp jumping on that fumble in the end zone, Damon Huard playing one of the best games of his career.

That defense had Warren Sapp and Ray Lewis. You could really tell Lewis was going to be good by watching him play that day.

But our offense really took it to them. There was a lot of purpose there that day—maybe because of what had happened in 1991. And it all helped to win that ballgame.

Stanford 2000 (Washington 31, Stanford 28)

Anybody who was there will never forget this game, which became much more than a game when Curtis Williams was injured late in the third quarter, an injury that cost him his life.

The play seemed freakish. It was hard to believe at first that it was that bad, because it seemed like a simple running play.

If you remember, Stanford had the ball deep near its own goal line late in the third quarter. Kerry Carter, now a member of the Seattle Seahawks, ran up the middle on first down. Curtis came up to make the tackle and met him head on.

You could tell something bad had happened from the way Curtis fell to the ground and the manner in which his teammates reacted. Still, it was hard to imagine what the end result would be.

Curtis ended up suffering a spinal cord injury that left him paralyzed from the neck down. He recovered well enough to make a trip back to Seattle for the 2002 spring game. But he died suddenly on May 6, 2002, two days after he had turned 24.

There hasn't been a more tragic story in UW football history.

I had gotten to know Curtis a bit from doing the Fox games and being around him. He was really the glue on the defense that year. You could tell the other guys on the team liked him. He was upbeat, and one of those guys to whom the other players on the team really gravitated. It reminded me of a bee hive, with Curtis in the middle of it and

Curtis Williams

everyone else buzzing around him on the outside. That's the kind of magnetic quality he had.

Curtis was also turning into a great player. I think he might have been as good a special teams player as we have ever had, particularly in covering punts and kickoffs. I still remember that on the play before he got hurt, Curtis downed a punt near Stanford's goal line.

Given what happened to Curtis, it's kind of hard to talk about the game itself. But even if Curtis hadn't gotten hurt, we'd still remember this one.

First there was the weather, which was a downpour by the end of the day. I remember standing on the field before the game and talking to Bill Diedrich, then a Stanford assistant who had worked at UW in the '90s. We were talking about the weather, and I said it was kind of warm and humid. He said that's a bad sign because that could turn into rain. It got so bad, you wondered how anybody could throw or catch the ball.

We led 24-6 midway through the fourth quarter. But then Stanford came back, scoring three TDs before we got the ball again thanks to recovering two on-side kicks.

We didn't think there was a way we could win the game then, considering what had happened with Curtis. But thankfully we had Marques Tuiasosopo. They still had to finish the ball game, they still had to play, and I credit Marques for getting the guys to be able to do that.

He led us right down the field in three plays, one of the most amazing drives I've ever seen. He just willed them to that win. Of all of Marques' comebacks at UW, that one had to be the most amazing.

Apple Cup 2002 (Washington 29, WSU 26, Three Overtimes)

What a bizarre game that was. I'd put it right up there with the 1975 Apple Cup for games that you walked away from unable to really fathom what had just happened. Thankfully, we were on the winning side each time.

What I remember most is Nate Robinson's interception, where he leaped over Mike Bush—who was 6'6" and also a basketball player in his spare time—to give us the ball deep in their territory late in the game. That allowed us to tie the game and send it into overtime, and once we were in overtime, it seemed like we had the momentum on our side, especially since Jason Gesser was sidelined.

Nate was amazing that year. He had gotten burned real bad earlier in the year against Cal and USC. But I had seen him play in high school, and I just knew that at some point in the season he was going to make a play that would make us say "wow." Just as he did later on the basketball court.

What I also remember is the look on Mike Price's face when the officials made that final call that we had recovered a backwards pass and the game was over. He had a dazed look, and he reminded me a little of Rodney Dangerfield, like "we get no respect."

Nate Robinson

Chapter 5

SOME OF MY FAVORITE PLAYERS

Steve Emtman

Well, putting Steve on this list was easy.

I never saw some of the guys from the earlier years who are acknowledged as the greats—Vic Markov, Chuck Carroll, Paul Schwegler, and on down the line.

But of the guys I've seen, Steve has to be at the top of the list as the best and most dominant player in Husky history.

Of all of Steve's great moments, two stand out for me.

One was the 1992 Rose Bowl when we beat Michigan to clinch the national title. There was a drive just before halftime where Michigan looked like it was getting ready to put points on the board. And Steve suddenly turned into a madman and absolutely destroyed their offensive line. There were two or three plays where he pushed them back and got to the QB, or got pressure on him and broke up the play. It was an awesome display, and

Steve Emtman

I remember Michigan coach Gary Moeller with a look of disbelief on his face. It seemed like at that moment, everyone knew the game was ours.

Then there was a game in 1990 against Arizona, right when that defense started to become incredibly dominant.

Arizona had a good running quarterback then named George Malauulu. They liked to use him on the option. Their first two plays of the game, Malauulu got the snap and couldn't take a step before Steve was right there, tackling him for big losses.

The crowd went crazy—some people said that was as loud as it's ever gotten at Husky Stadium—and we went on to beat them 54-10.

It's too bad Steve had all those injuries in the NFL, because I'm not sure if people outside of this area ever really got to see just how good he really was.

Michael Jackson

When Michael first got here, UW still had a junior varsity team. I remember going to a game one time and there he was playing tailback. And he looked really good, too. They knew he was really talented, but they were trying to figure out where to put him. They used him some at safety too before they finally put him at linebacker.

What a great move that turned out to be.

Of all the linebackers I've seen here, Michael might have had the best range. He could move from sideline to sideline, and then he could really hit you once he got there.

As important as Warren Moon was to that 1977 team, Michael was just as key. He had two games that year where he made 29 tackles—against Oregon State and Washington State—which are still tied for the school record. He also had an amazing 20 solo tackles against the Cougars that year—which is three more than any other player in school history has ever made in a game as this is written.

Michael Jackson

And then there was the interception in the final minute to clinch the Rose Bowl against Michigan.

I could go on, but you get the point.

He was a great competitor.

Ron Holmes

Ron Holmes

Here's how great Ron Holmes was. He played primarily defensive tackle during his time at UW, yet he once had five quarterback sacks in a game. He's second in UW history in tackles for a loss, which isn't easy to do from the tackle position.

When I think of that 1984 team that went 11-1, as much as anything I remember the defense—guys like Reggie Rogers, Jimmy Rodgers and Ron Holmes.

He was No. 90—boy, that's turned out to be a good one for us—and if you were a coach looking at game film of the Huskies, you always knew where he was.

Coaches always talk about linemen either having size but no speed, or vice versa. But Ron had both. I would have loved to have been a linebacker playing behind him. He made those guys look awfully good because he was clearing everybody out of the way up front.

There was no more fitting way for him to go out than that Orange Bowl against Oklahoma that year. I thought he was really key in offsetting their offense in that game.

Corey Dillon

Corey was only around for a year. But what a year he had in 1996. Nine 100-yard games. A Pac-10 record 22 touchdowns. A bunch of dominating performances.

And that game against San Jose State is still hard to believe. He had 222 yards rushing and an 83-yard reception for a touchdown—all in one quarter. I know San Jose State wasn't great that year. But I don't care if they had been the School of the Nuns. That was an awesome display.

There's a story I've heard that when Dillon got to the sidelines at the end of that quarter, he told a coach, "I'm done."

And while it might have been nice to see how many yards he really could have gotten that day—500 maybe?—his statement is true. What else could he have done?

I first saw Corey in high school when he was at Franklin High here in Seattle, and he was the epitome of the phrase "a man among boys." He looked like he could go straight to the pros at that point.

As well as that San Jose State game, however, I also remember Corey's games that year against Oregon and Washington State, when he got all kinds of tough yards, carrying three, four, five guys at one time. He looked like a magnet, because he'd run down the field and pick up guys as he was going.

Joe Steele

Joe, who played from 1976-79, was a really big recruit for Don James. He had been a star at Blanchet High and a lot of people wanted him. That was Don's first full recruiting class, and he was able to keep Joe at home,

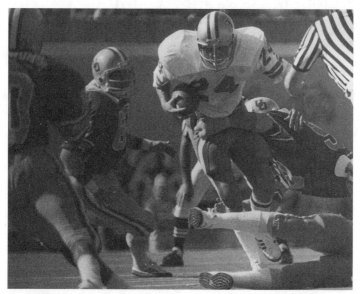

Joe Steele

which sent a signal to a lot of people about where Don was taking the Husky program.

Joe wasn't overly fast, but he was big and he ran on the front of his feet. Kind of a galloper. He ran heavy, and it seemed like he was always leaning forward, which allowed him to get another yard or two on every play.

But when he got outside on that sprint draw, he was usually gone. I can see him running that play over and over and over.

There will always be that "what if?" for Joe's career, however. He got hurt late in his last year in a game at UCLA when he was faking into the line and got hit on the knee. He was never the same after that. I think he would have had a nice career at the next level.

Calvin Jones and Bill Cahill

Any football program has a history of players who were bookends—players who seemed like they were almost brothers on the field, like Cliff (James Clifford) and Cloff (Dave Hoffman) from the 1991 national title team.

Calvin Jones, a cornerback, and Bill Cahill, a safety, were like that for the Husky teams I played on.

Both were purple helmet winners—the helmet players who had earned a special defensive status got to wear in practice and in games.

Nate Robinson has gotten a lot of attention the last few years for playing so well while listed at 5'9", though he may actually be an inch or two shorter.

Bill Cahill

Calvin Jones, however, was kind of Nate before Nate. He was also 5'9" and played with an infectious enthusiasm. He was always laughing, always smiling, always working hard.

And he had tremendous springs in his legs. He would many times knock down passes and make key tips on plays that seemed like they might be out of his range.

Calvin Jones

He and Bill also were dangerous punt returners—and back then, we could use them both at once. It was common in those days to have two punt returners. Now, it's almost impossible because of the punting alignments with the gunners lining up on each side of the field. Those guys have to be blocked, which really only leaves one guy left to return the kick.

It was nice to have them both back there doing it. They each went on to the NFL, and Bill returned a punt for a touchdown for the Buffalo Bills in the same game that O.J. Simpson went over 2,000 yards.

Calvin, though, wasn't exactly like Nate in one key way—he couldn't play basketball to save his life. He had the leaping ability to stuff a basketball. But he just couldn't play. We used to always laugh about that because it didn't seem to make sense given how great an athlete he was.

Ernie Janet

Ernie was a guard on the teams from 1968-70, and he was the toughest guy I played with.

He was part of a great offensive line that I was blessed to play with—I had Ernie, Bruce Jarvis at center, Wayne Sortun at tackle, Dan Cunningham at tackle, Lane Ronnebaum at guard.

But Ernie was the toughest guy. He was the first guy down field to knock someone down, and the first guy back in the huddle.

In practice, guys would run a play, and next thing they knew they were on their butt and wouldn't know where it came from. And it would be Ernie standing over them. He could get to the linebacker extremely quickly, and he knew how to deliver the blow. He could pull to get the safeties or take out the corners.

Ernie later played about four years in the NFL with the Bears and the Eagles, and I'm sure he was one of the toughest guys on those teams as well.

D'Marco Farr

When I think of D'Marco Farr I think of speed, not the *Best Damn Sports Show* or any of the other things he has become known for since he quit playing.

He had the body of a thoroughbred horse, like Secretariat, with a big muscular body. He didn't seem overly big up top, but you'd look at his legs and see that he had a great foundation speed.

I think I remember D'Marco best for a great game he had at Ohio State in 1993 when he made four tackles for a loss. He was a guy who could really make things happen.

Mark Lee

When you think of great cornerbacks, you're looking for guys who are tough, don't get beat deep, can come up and make the tackle, and have a short memory so they can quickly forget about it if something does happen.

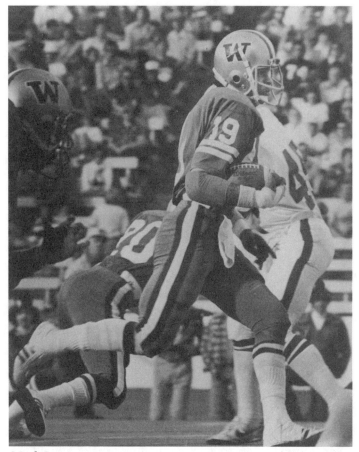

Mark Lee

Mark Lee was one of those guys, one of the best cornerbacks we've had here.

That gets forgotten sometimes, however, because of what a great punt returner Mark was. He had that incredible 1979 season when he returned three punts for touchdowns, including the one that beat Oregon.

The amazing thing about that was Mark wasn't the returner for every punt. We used Paul Skansi a lot that year as well. Some of that was because they knew Paul would make the catch. Sometimes coaches put guys in situations like that as much for what they won't do—such as fumbling—as for what they will do. But Mark was sure-handed and he also had that breakaway speed, and when there was a crucial situation late in the game, Mark was the guy.

Mario Bailey

Mario was the most acrobatic receiver I've ever seen play here.

I can remember a game at home where he laid himself completely flat out on the turf twice and came up with the catch. It was one of the most unbelievable things I've seen.

And who can forget the '92 Rose Bowl, when he caught that touchdown pass and then did the Heisman pose in the end zone, mocking Desmond Howard, who won the Heisman that year but didn't make any TDs in that game? That vividly illustrated the attitude that team had that year.

Mario might have been just a little too small to play in the NFL, although I think he would have been perfect for the Smurfs, the group that played for the Redskins in the '80s.

He was one of those guys you love as a quarterback because he would give up his body for the betterment of

Mario Bailey

the team. You get the ball in the vicinity of guys like that, and they are going to make you look good.

Lawyer Milloy

Lawyer, obviously, was one of the greatest of a long line of great safeties to play for us, and as I write this, he is still one of the best safeties in the NFL as well.

My one regret about Lawyer is that he has been distant from the program in recent years. We have to get him back into the program.

From what I understand, he harbored some ill feelings about what happened his last year, in 1995, when he was injured, and about whether he should have been playing or not. I think he thinks that hurt his chances of being drafted higher, and even though Lawyer is from Tacoma, he hasn't been around much since he left.

But he would be a great ambassador for the program as a local who made an instant impact, and I hope that he can get back into the program.

Tim Meamber

Tim was a linebacker on some of those great early 1980s teams—he topped more than 100 tackles in a season in 1982 and 1984—and a guy I first saw on the junior varsity. I always had a soft spot for him because he was from Yreka, California, which is about a half-hour from my hometown. You have to love those small-town guys who come to the big city and make it.

You also had to love the way Tim looked. He always reminded me of the big guy in Ichabod Crane, the big galoot kind of guy with the dimple in his chin and the big jaw. If you drew up on paper what a linebacker should look like, it would be Tim.

Dave Hoffman and James Clifford

These guys were great players on their own. But in Husky lore, they will always be together.

Cliff (James Clifford, naturally) and Cloff (Hoffman). The great defenders on the early '90s teams on the field and lovable and memorable characters off the field who both have gone on to great post-football success.

They really played the game together well on the field—Hoffman as the weak-side linebacker and Clifford on the inside. I thought they both played above their physical capabilities, something I think they would agree with if you asked them. And it's always fun to watch players who seem to be maximizing their ability.

Fittingly, they were the two leaders in tackles in 1992—their senior year—as Hoffman had 91 and Clifford had 82.

They then worked on the replays of Husky football games with me for a while, doing sideline reports together, and they were always insightful and a lot of fun. We wanted to keep them but we couldn't afford their salaries any more.

Each has gone on to much better things since then, however. Hoffman has gone on to work in the Secret Service, and Clifford played minor league baseball with the Mariners and is now a strength coach for them.

Jason Chorak

Maybe it didn't work out for Jason in the NFL as he would have liked and as a lot of us thought it would.

But you can't deny the year he had in 1996 when for one season he was one of the most feared defensive players we have had. He was named the Pac-10's Defensive Player of the Year that season—at this writing, the last Husky to win that award—and had 14.5 sacks, a school record. He also still holds the school record for tackles for a loss for a season (22) and for a career (59.5).

He was the perfect player for Jim Lambright's system as the quick and somewhat undersized pass rusher off the edge. He was tailor-made for that position, and maybe that hurt him when it came to the NFL since you have to have the size in that league.

He weighed only about 245 pounds or so during that 1996 season, which was his junior year. But he never let that stop him.

I remember watching him make an inside move on a tackle once and the guy grabbed his jersey. It looked like he was pulling it three yards as Jason tried to get away, and he was still able to make the tackle behind the line of scrimmage.

But he was fun to watch on just about every play, as he would battle with the tackle who was trying to hold him and strangle him and bringing that arm down.

I always thought he had the wrong image as being cocky. From my standpoint, doing the broadcasts for the replays, Jason was always great to interview.

Larry Triplett

Larry not only was one of the defensive stars of the 2000 Rose Bowl team, but he might also have been the nicest guy to ever play for us.

Whenever I'd see him at something he would always make sure to introduce me to his folks. He was impossible for anyone to ever root against if they got to know him. If you ever wanted a guy to be an ambassador for your school, it would be Larry.

Larry wasn't really a big numbers guy—of course, a lot of defensive tackles aren't. But Larry played at a time when we didn't have a lot of other dominant linemen, and Larry was always getting double-teamed. Still, it seemed like he was able to make a lot of plays, and the NFL obviously thought a lot of him since he's starting now for the Indianapolis Colts.

Mark Stewart

Mark was a linebacker for those early 1980s teams, just like Tim Meamber.

But the thing that stands out most for me about Mark is that he was the epitome of a student-athlete. He was one of the smartest guys to play for the Huskies and he did the work in the classroom, and it makes sense that he is now working in education and coaching high school football.

He also had one of the best games any UW linebacker has ever had in 1982 when he made 15 solo tackles in an intense games against UCLA—the winner took the inside track for the Rose Bowl—a mark that is still tied for third in school history. He also had five sacks in that game and was named *Sports Illustrated*'s National Player of the Week.

Mark was an All-American during his senior year in 1982 and his 47 career tackles for a loss were second in UW history as this was written.

Ray Horton

Ray played from 1979-82 and was a tremendous cover guy. It's like that moment in the movie *Hoosiers* when Gene Hackman tells one of his players that he wants to know what kind of gum the guy he's guarding is chewing. Ray would know.

He was from Tahoma High in Tacoma, one of long line of players from there at the time. His brother, Buddy, later became an official in the NFL.

Ray was also a great return guy at a time when our special teams were really something. His biggest play was probably a 73-yard punt return he had for a touchdown when we beat a No. 2-ranked USC team down at the L.A. Coliseum, the win that got us into the Rose Bowl that year.

Reggie Williams

Reggie was probably the biggest game-breaking receiver I've seen play for us.

Reggie Williams

He put up all kinds of numbers, and it helped that he played during an era when passing was more common and with a quarterback who could throw well like Cody Pickett. Those two were really lucky to have each other.

But I don't think we've ever had a receiver who had it all the way Reggie did—and the way he probably will in the NFL for a long time.

He has speed, hands, instincts and toughness. You could put him inside—like they did a lot in 2002 when he had three touchdowns against Oregon—or outside.

Reggie was another guy who I thought got something of a bad rap in terms of his image. I think a lot of people thought he was brash, and there's no question he's confident in his abilities, but he was also great to deal with during his time at UW.

Frank Garcia

Frank, who played guard and center from 1990-94, didn't become an All-American and didn't earn the honors that some of our other linemen have.

But to me, he was the epitome of nastiness, which is something every line—and football team—needs. And I don't mean in a dirty way. He just was one of those guys who was willing to do whatever it took to get the job done and didn't care if he made a few enemies on the other side along the way.

I can still see him in that stance with that helmet up a little and then bulling that neck forward and get getting after people. If I ever had to show a budding offensive linemen how to play the position, I'd find a tape of Garcia and put it on.

Olin Kruetz, who followed Frank as our center from 1995-97, was another guy in the same mold. You didn't want to make Olin mad, just like you didn't want to make Frank mad. And that kind of attitude is needed in football sometimes.

Napoleon Kaufman

Napoleon is still the leading rusher in school history and could be for a while, the way things are going these days with early entry and the like.

Napoleon almost left early himself, after his junior year in 1993, but decided to stick around for his senior season, in part because Jim Lambright told him he would do all he could to feature him in the offense. The school also built a big Heisman campaign around Napoleon, and it almost paid off. He was in the top three or so in the minds of most people until he got hurt late in the season and tapered off a bit.

But it worked for Napoleon when he was taken in the first round of the draft by the Raiders the next spring.

I remember we were doing the spring game that year on the same day as the draft and we had Lambo up in the press box doing some commentary. Napoleon had just found out he had been drafted, and he came over and embraced Lambo for like two or three minutes. It was really cool to see him thanking Coach Lambright for what he had done for him that season, making him the focus of the team and enabling him to be a first-round draft pick.

Jim got criticized by some other players at other times in his career, but as far as I could tell, Napoleon thought the world of him.

Napoleon was obviously one of the most exciting runners we have ever had. He broke a bunch of records held by Hugh McElhenny, and as of this writing, he holds the school record for most rushes of 50 yards or more—six.

Napoleon wasn't the biggest guy in the world, but he was so strong. I remember looking at him once and his arms were the size of a lot of people's calves. That obviously made it hard for tacklers to bring him down.

The other thing that always amazed me about him was that he always carried the ball in his left hand no matter what. He never switched it. I never understood how he could change directions, change sides of the field, and still keep holding the ball in his left hand.

I'm sure that's not how he was taught. But then, I'm not sure you'd really want to make a guy like him change anything.

Tommy Scott and Jimmy Kreig

I've got to end this with my two guys.

I don't mean to slight any other receivers with whom I played. They were all great in their own way.

But Tommy Scott and Jimmy Kreig were my two main guys.

People ask me all the time, "Who were your receivers, anyway?" and I'm always glad to tell them about Tommy and Jimmy.

Jimmy Kreig was the leading receiver on the 1970 team, the first year I was the starting quarterback, and caught 54 passes—a school record that lasted until Mario Bailey broke it in 1991—for 738 yards.

He was a junior college guy out of Taft in California, though he was originally from New York.

He had a tremendous burst off the line of scrimmage and had great speed as well as strong hands. He was recruited to return kickoffs, and he did that as well—he returned three kicks for touchdowns in his career, and two in 1970, both of which are still school records. But when they saw what great hands he had, he instantly became a starting receiver.

The next year, 1971, Jimmy was paired with Tommy Scott, who was another JC guy out of San Francisco.

Here's the amazing thing about Tommy—he played high school football in Daly City, which is basically a suburb of San Francisco, where he was teammates with Lynn Swann, whom I'm sure you all have heard of, and Jesse Freitas, who went on to play quarterback in the NFL. Imagine having three guys like that on one high school team.

Tommy became a big-play receiver for us almost immediately, catching 35 passes for 820 yards in 1971, an average of 23.4 yards per catch—no UW receiver has come close to that since then. The longest pass of my career went to Tom in 1972, a 72-yarder in a game against UCLA that was the final home game of our careers.

There was no more fitting way to go out.

I tell everybody I was blessed to play with receivers like those two guys who made me look that good.

Chapter 6

UNSUNG HEROES

Tommy Failla

Being able to expose a few more people to players like Tommy Failla is one of the main reasons I wanted to write a book like this.

Tommy was an All-Conference nose tackle in 1970—when he stood all of five feet, 11 inches and weighed all of 205 pounds. That will obviously never happen again.

That was my sophomore year—Tommy was a senior then—and he was such a leader on that team.

That was back when we had the "purple helmet" tradition. Defensive guys who got graded as playing at 100 percent or more by the coaches were rewarded with the purple helmet. They got to wear it in practices and in games, and when we were young guys, attaining that purple helmet was elite status. Anyone who wore it was really looked up to.

Tommy was one of those guys. You looked at him, watched him play and practice, and you knew he was a special player.

That's probably why he was able to make it even though he was so small.

In fact, it says in the 1970 media guide that "coaches at first thought there was no way he could play due to his lack of size, but he fooled everybody."

Interestingly, he was a halfback and quarterback in high school before coming to UW. Tommy didn't play professionally—his size surely became a factor there—but as a Husky, he was an All-Pro.

Scott Phillips

Scott was a wide receiver who came in right as I was leaving. He played from 1973-76, meaning he was there for the end of the Owens era and the beginning of the Don James era. He was a captain on that 1976 team and was another "little guy" who showed that heart and desire can overcome lack of height and weight.

Scotty was listed at five-ten and a half—when you're that size I guess you'll take every inch you can get—and when you saw him up close you said to yourself, "There's no way he's going to play football."

But Scotty, who was from Bellevue, was able to do more than play. He was the leading receiver for three straight years—from 1974-76—and as of 2003 was still sixth on the career receiving list with 111 catches.

It's too bad he graduated a year before the team went to the Rose Bowl, because he's one of those guys who really deserved it.

Beno Bryant

Here's another little guy made good—though no, you don't have to be a little guy who made good to make it on this list.

Beno was a running back for us from 1989-93, and getting him was a real sign that things were changing for us—top-notch talent from Los Angeles.

The story has always been that when Don James was recruiting Beno, who grew up in south central Los Angeles—a tough area of town—he heard an Uzi going off next door.

But whatever it took to get Beno was worth it.

Not only could he run, but he could return punts and do a lot of other things. He isn't really on any of the top 10 career lists, but I remember him as a guy who was always dependable and willing to do what needed to be done for some of our greatest teams.

Paul Skansi

Maybe Paul Skansi doesn't belong on a list of unsung players. I mean, he was our leading career receiver until Reggie Williams passed him.

Paul Skansi

And he played all those years for the Seahawks, which kept him in the public eye.

Still, I think sometimes when people remember that 1981 Husky team that won the Rose Bowl, they think of Jacque Robinson rushing for all those yards, or Steve Pelluer playing a steady quarterback.

But I think Paul was just as big a part of it as anybody else.

He always reminded me a little of Scott Phillips in that he wasn't overly big—he was 5'11", 190. And unlike Scott, he wasn't overly fast. He wasn't going to make you miss and head out on a 90-yard TD run or something.

But when you needed a tough catch in traffic, he was your guy.

One of the toughest catches he ever made was in the 1981 Apple Cup, the game that decided who would go to the Rose Bowl that year. WSU led 7-3 late in the first half, but we were driving. With eight seconds left in the first half, he made an incredible diving catch of a Pelluer pass for a touchdown that seemed to turn the momentum of the game around. A lot of people thought a WSU defensive back named Nate Bradley might be in position to intercept the ball—and maybe run 100 yards the other way—but Skansi outmaneuvered him to get the ball instead.

Paul was always a quiet, unassuming kind of guy, but he was the kind of guy you always need in your program.

Willie Hurst

Willie was a running back from 1998-2001 and one of the stars of the 2000 team that beat Purdue in the Rose Bowl. In fact, he scored the clinching touchdown of that Rose Bowl win.

Interestingly enough, Rick Neuheisel had tried to make a receiver out of him earlier that spring, even though Willie already had a pretty good track record as a running back. In 1998, he had set the school freshman rushing record.

But you could see why some people might have been fooled by Willie.

He had what you would call "football speed." He couldn't run a whole lot faster than you and me if it was just lining up and doing 40s. I remember when he first got to UW. On freshman timing day, he ran a 4.7 40-yard dash. A lot of people wondered what kind of running back we had gotten.

But put Willie on a football field and he had a way of making people miss. He just really elevated himself.

And he was also like Marques Tuiasosopo in that he had a way of elevating everyone else around him as well.

He was one of those guys in the locker room who everyone else would listen to and follow and take them with him to another level. I think it was pretty evident once Willie was gone how much he had meant to the team.

Willie Hurst

Mark Jerue

Mark Jerue was a linebacker from 1978-81 who was a co-captain of the 1981 team that won the Rose Bowl.

He was also one of those great recruiting stories that only seems to happen in college football.

The Huskies had just one scholarship left in the winter of 1977 and were trying to decide between Mark—who had been a standout at Mercer Island—and a big kid named Gary Patrick out of Yakima.

I know all about this because Gary is my brother-in-law's brother-in-law. Gary's father was a diehard Husky fan and he really wanted to go to Washington.

But Don James decided to take Mark Jerue and Mark ended up having a great career—he was an All-Pac-10 linebacker in 1981 and had 330 tackles, which as I write this is second since 1967 among all players who were defensive linemen for most of their career. Mark was a nose guard until his senior year.

But Gary Patrick had a good career as well. He ended up at Washington State and became a starting offensive lineman—meaning he and Mark had to battle a few times in Apple Cups.

I'm glad we took Mark, but I wish we could also have taken Gary.

John Fiala

John Fiala was as true a Husky as there has ever been. How so?

Well, consider that he turned down a scholarship offer to USC to attend Washington, instead. John grew up in Bellevue and became a huge Husky fan and simply decided he wanted to be a Husky no matter what, so he decided it was worth paying his own way, even if other schools were willing to pay his way for him. The story is that John had a somewhat disappointing senior year at Lake Washington High so the Huskies decided he wasn't worth a scholarship. And USC was the school his mom had attended, so he had a tie-in there.

But then John walked on, and he had earned a scholarship by the time he was a sophomore and was our leading tackler as an insider linebacker as a senior in 1996. He then went on to a pretty lengthy NFL career, showing once again just how inexact a science recruiting is.

Ed Cunningham

Ed was the center on the 1991 national title team. Though if you saw him today, you'd never know he ever played college football, let alone five years in the NFL. He must weigh about 180 pounds now at the most.

But Ed was 6'3", 285 when he centered the line at UW. That was a really great line in 1991. Lincoln Kennedy, who went on to play more than a decade in the NFL, was the real star at one tackle spot. There was also Pete Kaligis and Kris Rongen and Siupeli Malamala. Those five guys all started all 12 games that year, one reason that team was able to have such a magical season.

But I thought Ed was the guy who held it all together. He wasn't the biggest guy or the fastest guy, but he was a smart player. I thought Malamala was really a great guy and very talented, but wasn't always motivated, and I think Ed was able to push Malamala to get more out of him.

I really liked Lincoln Kennedy, too. He was kind of like Nate Robinson in that he was always smiling and he played with flair, which is hard to do when you're an offensive tackle. I've always thought if you got Lincoln Kennedy and Nate Robinson together, they'd look like that movie *Twins* with Arnold Schwarzenegger and Danny DeVito. Two guys who could be brothers but are so different physically.

Joe Jarzynka

Joe might have been one of the most popular players of his time.

How could you not like a 5'7", 175-pound walk-on with long hair flowing out of the back of his helmet? Joe was so popular he had his own fan club for a while.

But Joe was more than a novelty act.

In 1998, he was the most valuable player on the team, playing receiver, returning kicks and even serving as the field goal kicker at the end of the season.

I remember the first time Jarzynka kicked a field goal in one of the games we were doing and Kevin Calabro, the voice of the Seattle Sonics who was doing play-by-play, called him "Joe the Toe." Other fans I knew called him "Shoeless Joe."

A lot of people thought it was kind of a joke that Joe was the field goal kicker that year, and certainly it wasn't ideal. But Joe made 6-8 field goals including a 44-yarder in bad weather in Pullman to help beat the Cougars.

One thing about Joe, once you met his parents you didn't wonder how he turned out the way he did. Sometimes you meet the parents of a lineman and they're each 5'10" or something. But with Joe, his parents looked exactly like he did.

Jay Roberts

Since I've been a part of Husky football, we have always prided ourselves on special teams. There are all kinds of games that people can point to that were won almost solely by the special teams, such as the incredible win over USC in 1981 when Fred Small recovered a botched kickoff in the end zone for the only touchdown of the game.

To me, one of the greatest special teams players we ever had was Jay Roberts, who lettered three times in the mid-80s. Jay became kind of a cult hero because he would race down the field on kickoffs and just lay someone on the other team out.

I've talked to more Husky fans through the years who said they didn't want to be late to a game because they didn't want to miss Jay Roberts on the kickoff team. Now that says something.

Jay was an interesting story even before he started becoming a special teams standout.

He was a great football and baseball player in Centralia and signed with UW and was also drafted in the first round by the Atlanta Braves. He signed with the Braves and played four years in their organization, but didn't make it to the big leagues.

So in 1984, he decided to come back to college. He walked on at UW and earned a letter as both a linebacker and a special teams player. The record shows that he never started any games for us. But the record doesn't show what an exciting player he was to watch.

The Tight End Position

In 1998, *Sports Illustrated* did some interesting research where they tried to determine which schools were the best at producing players at each position for the NFL.

Washington was chosen as the most prolific at producing tight ends.

So I figured that the whole position deserved its own section, starting with the era when I played.

The First Great Ones

I always made sure I knew where my tight end was in the route system, because he's the guy you are going to look to if everything else breaks down. He's the guy who can still bail you out and get some positive yards if your first options are covered.

I remember when I was a kid in Ashland watching the Huskies on TV and seeing Dave Williams play. He was a big guy who was also a track guy, and he scored 10 touchdowns one season. Because he was a track guy, he could really jump and go get the football, and that's not something you always see in a tight end. He ended up playing seven seasons in the NFL as a wide receiver and is really the beginning of UW's great tight end tradition.

I was lucky when I played that we had two great tight ends—Ace Bulger and John Brady. Ace was a 6'4", 230-pounder from Tacoma whom we used a lot that season.

Brady was the same year I was and became the starter in 1971 and 1972 after Ace had left.

John wasn't as big as Ace, but he had great hands and he put up some big numbers for a tight end at that time. As a junior he averaged 17.2 yards per catch, and as a senior he had 30 catches and 450 receiving yards. He left school with 67 catches, which stood for almost 15 years as the school record for a tight end.

John ended up getting drafted in the third round by the Detroit Lions, and I used to always tease him that I helped him get a pro contract. He still sends me a Christmas card every year, but there's never a check inside. Just the card. Oh well.

The Position Takes Off

After those two guys, it wasn't really until Don James took over that the tight end position really became a key part of the passing offense again.

Scott Greenwood and David Bayle were each key parts of teams from 1976-80, and then Tony Wroten became the guy in the early '80s.

But the first great receiving tight end after John Brady was probably Rod Jones, who caught a then school-record 75 passes as a tight end from 1984-86.

Rod was another of those guys who just looked like a football player. He had those long legs and those big arms, and he ended up playing three years in the NFL, including a year with the hometown Seahawks.

And essentially, from that year on, there has been a great tight end on the roster every year since, from Aaron Pierce to Mark Bruener to Ernie Conwell to Cam Cleeland to Reggie Davis to Jerramy Stevens to Kevin Ware. Every single one of those guys played in the NFL.

In fact, the position has been so loaded that one guy who started just one game in his career—Jeremy Brigham—was drafted and played six years in the NFL, including a Super Bowl.

My Favorites

Of all the tight ends I remember watching, I think Mark Bruener, who played from 1991-94 and was still in the NFL when this was written—stands out above the rest of them.

When he showed up in 1991, just in time to be on the national title team, he seemed so mature for his age. He really had a grasp of what he was trying to do and how to go about being a college football player. And he did more than just see bit time that year as a true freshman. He caught a key touchdown pass in the Rose Bowl win over Michigan that sewed up the national title, tightroping along the back of the end zone as he pulled the ball down. Mark is the leading tight end receiver in school history with 90 catches.

The other tight end up there is Aaron Pierce, who played from 1988-91.

He was maybe the best combination of being big and able to block and run and catch the ball.

Conwell, who is also still in the NFL as this is written, was maybe the strongest tight end we have ever had.

When you look at all these guys and what they produced, it isn't just in the TD passes they caught, but it's also all the little catches they had, the third-down receptions to keep a drive alive. That's what has made the position so key for us through the years.

When I look through the list, one guy who really epitomizes the position is Kevin Ware, who played from 1999-2002. He was a guy who had to sit and wait his turn behind Jerramy Stevens and really had just one year to make his mark. And then he makes 42 catches as a senior and lands in the NFL. It was like the light finally went on and he was able to take advantage of the opportunity he had.

My Favorite Kickers

For a long time, our other real hallmark position was placekicker, especially during the Don James era.

And the three kickers who stand out the most to me were all from Don's time—Jeff Jaeger, Mike Lansford and Chuck Nelson.

Lansford was a JC transfer who played on the 1978 and 1979 teams who still holds the UW record for never missing an extra point. He also had a really strong leg and went on to a long career in the NFL with the Los Angeles Rams.

Chuck was phenomenally accurate, making 30 in a row from November 14, 1981, to November 20, 1982—which as this was written was still an NCAA record for consecutive field goals.

Chuck Nelson

And they weren't all gimmes, either. Two of the kicks were 49-yarders, and the streak started in that memorable 1981 game at home against USC when the winds were about 60 miles per hour.

It's too bad that Chuck is often remembered primarily for that one miss against Washington State in 1982.

The thing I like best about Chuck is what an ambassador he is for the university. I've always really admired all he does in the community and the way he handles himself.

Jeff, meanwhile, was amazingly productive. His 80 field goals were also an NCAA career record as this was written. Jeff also set an NCAA record by making 19-23 field goals from 40-49 yards.

That Jeff made so many field goals showed how much confidence Don had in him. It might also indicate how much trouble we had scoring touchdowns in the red zone for a year or two there. But I prefer to think it was just that Don thought it was better off to be conservative and send Jeff out there.

One thing about all those kickers, they were all walkons, which is how Don did it back then. He didn't want to spend a scholarship on an unproven kicker, thinking instead that he would entice guys to walk on and then give them scholarships once they had proven themselves. It worked great for a while. But after Spokane's Jason Hanson—who was still in the NFL as this was written—went to Washington State because they offered him a scholarship, Don decided to change and gave a scholarship to Jason's younger brother, Travis.

It's worth noting that it's gotten harder to kick now, as well. The goal posts were wider back then and they could also use a tee. I also remember that in my day, the uprights were lower, which made it harder, I think, for the kickers to aim, and harder for the officials to judge kicks that went high over the goal posts. I think that hurt kickers of my era a little bit. The hash marks were also further out in my day, which made the angles a little tougher for kickers. Maybe it's best to say that it's all evened out, and a good kicker of that era would still be a good kicker today.

Punters

Unfortunately, we haven't had quite as much success with punters as with kickers, historically. Not sure what it is. All the excuses you could make, such as the swirling winds, the rainy weather, etc., would seem to affect field goal kickers as well. But for whatever reasons we've had a lot of luck with the kickers and not with the punters.

Two punters that stand out to me are Skip Boyd, who was a couple of years younger than me and became an All-American in 1974. He had a 43.0 yard average in 1973 that was still the best in UW history as this was written.

Skip was from Chelan, and he was a big guy. That gave him a lot of power and also great hang time.

The other punter I'd mention is Rich Camarillo, who was another JC guy who punted in 1979 and 1980. It's kind of funny that Rich's numbers with us weren't that great. He averaged only 37.9 yards per punt as a senior in 1980, which is one of the lower averages any of our punters have had in the last 25 years.

But obviously he had a strong leg, because he went on to kick in the NFL for 15 years. Just goes to show that your college stats don't always indicate what you will do in the pros.

Bobby Jarvis and Mark Drennan

I thought I would end this chapter by talking about two guys I played with who each ran into tragedy. Bobby, who played running back, was a member of the "Red Raiders." That's what we called the players who were red-shirting. Bobby was one of the toughest of those guys. Even though he never really played, he stood out because of how tough he played on those Red Raider teams. Kind of like the Rudy of the Red Raiders. After he was done playing, he lost both his legs and his arm in a construction accident.

But he didn't let that stop him. He went on to have a successful career running a boxing facility in the Rainier Beach area of Seattle. One of the best things about Bobby was that he didn't let the accident change him.

All of us who know him laugh and say that he was an ornery old cuss before the accident and he was an ornery old cuss after the accident.

Mark Drennan was a promising young wide receiver from California with a load of natural talent and great leaping ability. Unfortunately he was killed in an auto accident involving a drunken driver in 1971.

Washington still has awards named after each of them—the Bob Jarvis Award is given each year to the most inspirational walk-on; the Mark Drennan Memorial Award is given each year to the Defensive Scout Squad MVP.

But I just hope each year when the awards are given that people understand who these two players were. They are the kind of guys who sometimes get forgotten. But they shouldn't be.

Chapter 7

FRIENDS AND RIVALS

The Big Rivals

When I played, and going farther back to Hugh McElhenny's day, the big game of the year was always USC. Every time the schedule came out, you'd look and find when that game was going to be played.

And back in my day, the USC game down there was always a nighttime affair in the L.A. Coliseum, so that was fun no matter what. And they were the school you wanted to beat the most because they were the name program at the time—the team that was always in bowl games, the school with a lot of money, the team that was always on ABC. We used to always joke that whoever ran ABC must be a USC alum because they were on TV so much.

I just wish we had beaten them. We lost 28-25 my sophomore year down there and 13-12 my junior year at home, two of the toughest defeats we had.

Just behind beating USC was beating Northwest rivals. We didn't call it the Northwest Championship back then—Rick Neuheisel came up with that a few years ago. We always talked about beating them; we just didn't put a name to it.

We had pretty good success doing that when I was in school—we went 3-0 against Oregon State and 2-1 against Oregon and Washington State.

I always thought the UW-WSU game was the most fun when it was played in Seattle because there is such a huge contingent of graduates in the city who went to either UW or WSU. It seems like almost everybody went to one school or the other. It's not the same in California, where all the Cal or Stanford grads don't end up hanging around the Bay Area.

It's funny because I meet a lot of people now who are WSU grads and they are almost apologetic in a way. They say "Sonny, sorry, but I went to Washington State," like they feel bad about it when they meet me. But I always tell them, you don't have to apologize to me. You have to be true to your school. That's the way it's supposed to be. And that's what makes the rivalry so great.

The 1964 Rose Bowl

One of the coolest things that happened to me was getting to meet and talk with Dick Butkus a few years ago. Not only was Dick an NFL legend, but he was also a star for the Illinois team that played the Huskies in the 1964 Rose Bowl.

Bob Schloredt

I've always thought that 1963 team gets a little lost. People always remember the 1959 and 1960 teams that won back-to-back Rose bowl games and had Bob Schloredt at quarterback and all of that. And then they remember all the teams that went to the Rose Bowl in recent years.

But the 1963 team deserves to be remembered as well. It rallied from an 0-3 start to win six of its last seven games and clinch a Rose Bowl berth.

Butkus said his Illinois team that year had a knack for winning the close games—10-7, 6-3, scores like that.

He told me that when they got to the Rose Bowl, all they heard about was Rick Redman, the All-American lineman for us, and Bill Douglas, our quarterback.

He told me that they decided that Douglas was the key to the game, that the Huskies weren't quite as good without him as they were with him. He said they weren't really gunning for him necessarily, but they wanted to make sure he got an extra hit once in a while.

It happened quickly. UW drove down the field deep into Illinois territory. On a first down play, Douglas scampered up the middle on quarterback keeper to Illinois' 12-yard line. And then he didn't get up, being taken off the field on a stretcher with an injury, done for the day.

I don't know for sure if Butkus was the one who knocked him out, but listening to him talk about it that day, it wouldn't be a surprise.

And he was right. UW was different without Douglas as Illinois went on to win 17-7, holding the Huskies to just 183 yards.

Dee Andros

Dee was the legendary coach at Oregon State and one of my favorite opposing coaches.

I'll never forget the first time we played them and here came this guy dressed in a gigantic orange sweatshirt. We understood immediately why they called him "The Great Pumpkin."

Oregon State was one of the schools I grew up watching, especially once they had Bill Enyart, who was from Medford. I took a recruiting trip there, but Dee told me that he didn't think I was big enough to compete at the Pac-8 level. They wanted me to go to a junior college for a while so I might grow a little bit.

At least, that's how I remember it.

A few years later, we were both at a banquet. Dee got up to speak and he told a story about how he tried his darndest to recruit me—boy did he really want me, he said—but in the end I turned him down and went to Washington.

I just had to laugh, because that's not even close to how I remember it.

But I also had to laugh because Dee was really one of those guys who could light up a room when he spoke. Kind of like Jim Walden, the longtime coach at Washington State. Don James once joked that he felt like he was a "2,000-word underdog" against Jim Walden. He probably would have been about as big an underdog against Dee.

It was funny, too, that when he was recruiting me, he wore this giant black windbreaker. So I didn't really know what the whole Great Pumpkin thing was all about until I saw him run on the field that day.

Don McKeta

When I first got to Washington, I heard a lot about Don McKeta, who was a running back on the 1959 and 1960 teams that won the Rose Bowl. I heard all about the play he made against Oregon in 1960 when he caught a ball near the sideline late in the game and faked out an Oregon defensive back named Dave Grayson—who played in the NFL for a long time. McKeta pretended he was about to go out of bounds, then raced around Grayson and dashed into the end zone for a touchdown to win the game.

It's one of the most memorable plays in Washington history, with the fact that it came against the Ducks making it that much better. We heard stories that he had a gash in his leg that day and was in all kinds of pain. But he was from the old school that said if you could walk, you would to play.

When I met him for the first time, I kept looking at him because I'd heard so many stories about how tough he was. I was in awe of him then, and I have to admit that I'm still in awe of him when I see him today. That's how much of an effect he had on me.

Don is indicative of what the old-style Huskies were like and what people mean when they talk about Husky football.

Don McKeta

Another guy I really admire is Dave Kopay, who was one of the captains of the 1963 team that went to the Rose Bowl and then later was one of the first pro athletes to admit he was gay.

I think that took a lot of courage for him to do that and said a lot about what he was as a player and who he is as a person.

Bill Bissell

The year I arrived at UW was also the first year that Bill Bissell was Washington's marching band director. And I can't tell you how much of an impact Bill made on the marching band, which helped turn Husky football into such an event during that time and until he retired in 1993.

I've always been one of those who think that college football is about so much more than just the game itself, and Bill was one of those unforgettable guys who added so much to it. He attacked everything he did with such fun and creativity, whether it was having the band re-create the Mount St. Helens explosion or wearing bizarre costumes. There was the one time I remember when we played the Oregon Ducks, he pulled out a shotgun like he was going duck hunting, and the entire band fell to the ground. He helped turn "Louie, Louie" and "Tequila" into songs that became closely associated with our school. It didn't feel like a Husky football game without hearing them.

Robb Weller

I was just as fortunate to be a player when Robb Weller—who later went on to a TV career as the host of *Entertainment Tonight*—was our yell leader.

Robb was so good that if we were way ahead in a game, a lot of us would turn around and listen to what Weller was saying instead of paying attention to the game. To pass the time before the game, he used to do things like bring an issue of *Playboy* and read questions and answers from the *Playboy* Advisor. I remember during our 1970 rout of UCLA—the Payback Game for UCLA pouring it on us the year before—he was mocking UCLA's quarterback, Dennis Dummit, the whole game, yelling, "Fumble, damn it, Dummit, fumble, Dummit, damn it." A lot of us when we think of that game remember that cheer as much as anything.

Robb was so good that in 1972, my senior year and the year everyone thought we would make it to the Rose Bowl, they brought him back to be the yell leader even though he had already been the yell leader for four years.

A few years later, in 1981, Robb and Bill Bissell cooked up the cheer that turned into The Wave, which soon became a nationwide craze. The Washington football media guide gives credit to Robb for inventing The Wave during a win over Stanford in 1981 as the Huskies scored 28 straight points in the second half.

Others have tried to take credit for the wave. But us Huskies know Robb was the real inventor.

Broadcasting

I've dabbled a bit in broadcasting since my playing days were done and enjoyed it. Most notably, I began working in 1994 as the color analyst for the TV replays that most recently have been shown on Fox Sports Net.

Chuck Nelson did them before me but moved up to doing the analysis for the radio broadcasts, and that opened up a spot for me.

I guess I've done okay, because I've had some people suggest that I should try to do some other things, maybe live games on Fox or some other network. But that's not what I want do to. I got involved in it because I was excited to do Husky football and stay around the program a little bit. I have no other aspirations for it. I don't want to travel.

It's not always as glamorous a job as it might seem, however. I did some high school games in the '80s, and doing some of these broadcasts sometimes reminds me of those days. When you are the visiting team, you aren't exactly the first priority for the hosts—they don't really open up their arms to you all the time. For instance, the times we've been in Miami to do games at the Orange Bowl, we've been on the roof of the press box, outside in the humidity. You can barely see the jersey numbers from there. In some places, you get stuck in a little room in the press box way down at one end. You can get put in some pretty awkward spots, and it makes for some challenges.

But it's a lot of fun to do, and I hope to do it as long as they'll have me.

Legends

One of the greatest things they've done at UW in recent years is institute the Legends Program, where former players and coaches are honored at the end of the third quarter of a game at Husky Stadium.

Trust me, it really means a lot to be recognized.

It's even better now that they have the HuskyTron and they can show career highlights and all of that.

Another great thing is the Lucky Dawg program, where a young fan from the Children's Hospital or the Fred Hutchinson Cancer Research Center walks on the field with the team captains for the coin flip before the games.

When I played, we didn't have an organized program like that. But I remember my senior year they had a young man flown up from California who was dealing with a kidney problem. He was a really big fan of the team, no more than eight or nine years old, and I remember that he had the headbands and T-shirts and the whole bit.

The point is that those are the kind of things you still remember all these years later, being able to do a little something to make someone else feel good.

Bruce King

Bruce King was the No. 1 sports TV broadcaster in Seattle during my playing days, and he also hosted the *Jim Owens Show* on Sunday afternoons, which was a replay of the previous day's game with comments from the coach.

And I can't impress upon you enough what a big deal that was at the time.

Every Sunday, once our meetings and other appointments were done, we all raced to find a TV to watch the show and hear what Coach Owens had to say.

I always felt like he downplayed some of our accomplishments a little bit in kind of the typical coaches' style of not wanting to go really crazy in applauding you when you did something well.

And then there were other times he would criticize us, and we'd all look at the TV and say, "You're kidding me, right?"

The replay show that we do now is kind of the same thing. But that show was great because it was a true coach's show, with Coach Owens talking throughout the whole hour.

Bruce also used to show an interview with the coach of the opposing team every Friday night before a home game. We would always watch that on the 11 o'clock news, and then it would be lights out after that.

We always had it in the back of our mind that Bruce was a big-time part of UW football. So were some of the other media characters from that time, such as Emmett Watson, the longtime columnist for both the *P-I* and the *Times*, and Royal Brougham and Phil Taylor, who were also with the *P-I*. I always felt like all of those guys were fans of mine, and it was much appreciated.

Bob Robertson

Believe it or not, the man who has become known in the Pacific Northwest as the voice of Washington State University football was actually the voice of the Huskies the first two years I played for the team. Bob worked for KVI, which had the rights to UW games at the time, so Robertson did our games, and I remember him doing a great job.

But after the 1971 season, the rights to UW games were bought by another station. Robertson stayed at KVI, which took over Washington State games, and he has been with the Cougars ever since. It's funny to think that he might never have done WSU games if the rights hadn't changed.

I see Bob all the time nowadays, and we reminisce about all the great games of those two years and all the ups and downs. The thing I liked so much about Bob is that he was always around. He seemed to really want to get to know the players and was so professional about it, and that really came through in his broadcasts.

I think he even had the same trademark saying then that he has now, about always being a good sport, being a good sport always.

Back then, he was a big part of Husky football, even if he would probably never want to admit that now.

Then and Now

As I finish this, I think about all the changes in college football from the time I played until now.

I look around the athletic facilities at Washington and am just amazed. Now there's a weight room seemingly big enough to park a 747 inside. When I played, we had a weight room underneath the Tubby Graves Building that wasn't even big enough for all of us to be inside at once. You had to take a number to wait your turn.

I remember that it was after we played a game at Texas A&M in 1987 and saw their facilities that a bunch of our alumni got serious and decided we needed to do some upgrades here.

The players themselves are so much different. Bigger, stronger, faster. In my day, if you had a big guy on your team, it usually meant he was overweight and trying to hide his belly. These days, the kids are just gigantic, and there's nothing fat about them at all.

One of the best differences, I think, is the help the athletes get these days in the classroom. I know there's a lot of criticism sometimes of what schools do to help the players academically. But I look back at what we did and what I know they do today, and they get so much more help. There's much more of an emphasis on it today, making sure you are successful in the classroom. It wasn't that way at all when I played.

And the kids get outside help as well. We pretty much had practice and that was it. Now there are camps and private tutors and clinics and all of that stuff, which to be honest, I'm not sure really matters all that much. I've never heard one kid say that all that other stuff he paid for helped him any more than the training he got at the university.

But the one thing that really hasn't changed is what it means to be a Husky.

Running down the tunnel on game day. Feeling the Husky Stadium stands shake in anticipation of a great defensive play. Sharing in the joy of victories past, present and future.

It's still as great to be a Husky now as it was then.

EPILOGUE

After my UW career ended in 1972, I was signed as a free agent by the Los Angeles Rams after I was not taken in the NFL draft. I guess they didn't like my size. But I was cut pretty early into camp.

That, however, provided an opening for one of the more interesting moments in my life.

In 1970, while I was a sophomore at UW, I met Burt Reynolds.

I remember one day, our sports information director, John Reid, told me that he had gotten a call and Reynolds was in town and wanted to know if he could meet me. I remember getting taped for practice, and here comes Burt and his entourage. He said hello to a lot of the guys and hung out for a while. That's where it got started that he had Cherokee in him. I was Cherokee, and that's why he had wanted to meet me, because he had an eighth Cherokee in him.

After that, he used to write us a letter every year asking us to have dinner at his house when we played in Los Angeles. But you can't really do that on a trip to play a game, so we never did.

But getting to know Burt paid off for me. After I was cut by the Rams, I got a call from Burt and an invitation to act in a movie he was making called *The Longest Yard*.

It was a no-brainer to accept that invitation. When I got cut, it was too late to get into fall quarter at Washington, so I said I'd do the movie.

But for a little while, I was wondering what I'd gotten myself into. I had to fly to Savannah, Georgia, and when I got there, there was nobody there to meet me. I finally had to get a cab to drive me 100 miles to Glenville, where the movie was being filmed. I walked into the hotel and there were some guys watching *Monday Night Football*. I said, "Who's in charge here?" and Ray Nitschke pointed to a woman, who wrote a check for the cab.

Also on the set was Joe Kapp, who was only a few years removed from leading the Minnesota Vikings to the Super Bowl.

Some days we would hang out at Burt Reynolds's house and Dinah Shore would cook lunch for us. I remember, when that was going on, that my mom just loved Dinah Shore, and here I was sitting on the couch with her like she's family.

It sure seemed like a long way from Ashland, Oregon, right about then.

Even though *The Longest Yard* was a great experience—I still get a small royalty check every year—I didn't think I was done playing football and I wanted to get back in the game.

I had a lot of people trying to help me.

At one point, Burt called Howard Cosell on my behalf to see if he could help me get back into the NFL

That didn't work.

Neither did going to Canada, though I gave it a brief try.

In 1974, I signed with the Toronto Argonauts in what turned out to be a big mistake. They were a horrible team with a horrible coach—John Rauch, the same guy who decided that O.J. Simpson should be used as a decoy and not actually given the ball when he was with the Buffalo Bills just a few years earlier.

The Argonauts had just lost Joe Theismann to the NFL and were looking for somebody to replace him. Joe had done a great job in Toronto, and they couldn't get over those days. It was just a bad scenario for me all the way around. I got cut and then a couple weeks later they fired Rauch.

But football kept calling. I played briefly for the Philadelphia Bell of the World Football League—remember that league?—and after that, an owner for a team in Hawaii called and asked if I would be interested in playing there.

I wasn't sure, but they said they'd fly me over for a few days, so I went and the next thing I know, they're making me an offer. I got there the second week of practice and ended up starting and sharing the QB duties with Rick Cassata, who became a good friend of mine.

I got a house out in Hawaii Kai and had a lot fun—how could playing football in Hawaii be anything else?

One of the great things about the WFL was playing with some guys who had been big names in the NFL.

One was Ken Bowman, who had been the center for the Green Bay Packers. It was great getting together with guys like that and watching films of old games.

Another NFL vet on that team was Calvin Hill, who had just won a Super Bowl with the Dallas Cowboys.

He had his three-year-old son with him, Grant. You might have heard of him.

Anyway, Grant was big for his age, as would probably be evident in hindsight. But at the time, a lot of the guys on the team just thought he was another kid. He was so big that a lot of guys figured he must be five or six years old.

Little did we know.

Another interesting character there was Duane Thomas, who had played with Hill for the Cowboys and was trying to stay in football after having basically been kicked out of the NFL.

We'd all heard the stories about Duane, and we all thought he was a little different. He'd wear suits every single day. "Man, you're in Hawaii and you're wearing a suit? What's wrong with this guy?"

I had a great time there, probably the best experience of my pro career given that I got to play some and we were in Hawaii. We also helped open the stadium there, Aloha Stadium, where the Huskies have since returned several times to play bowl games.

But as you might imagine, we had just horrible road trips. I remember one game we played in Jacksonville. We flew to Los Angeles and laid over. Then we had a stop in Texas before we got to Jacksonville.

Then we stayed there and flew to Philadelphia for a game at old Franklin Field.

Then we flew to Portland for a week before playing a game there, and then we went home.

That meant we were on the road for three weeks with all these players, coaches and managers. And we didn't stay at cheap hotels.

No wonder the league went bankrupt.

That happened a few weeks later and a lot of us got taken. I ended up getting 30 cents on the dollar for the rest of my contract.

That was better than some guys, who didn't get enough money to fly home.

Calvin Hill had the biggest contract, and they weren't going to pay him at all until his agent threatened to have the books of one of the owners opened. All of the sudden, Calvin got paid.

I had one last chance to play, signing with the San Diego Chargers in 1976.

But I was struggling with a torn rotator cuff—an injury I still have today—and it just wasn't going to happen. I ended up electing not to even go down there and embarrass myself.

And that was it with football.

I returned to Seattle to get a job and I've never left.

Kind of like Husky football, which came to Seattle in 1889 and will stay forever.

Celebrate the Heroes of Washington Sports
and Professional Football in These Other Releases from Sports Publishing!